Weight Training Basics

Weight Training Basics

Robert Kennedy

Sterling Publishing Co., Inc. New York

Library of Congress Cataloging-in-Publication Data Available

10 9 8 7 6 5 4 3 2 1

Published by Sterling Publishing Company, Inc..
387 Park Avenue South, New York, N.Y. 10016
© 1997 by Robert Kennedy
Distributed in Canada by Sterling Publishing
c/o Canadian Manda Group, One Atlantic Avenue, Suite 105
Toronto, Ontario, Canada M6K 3E7
Distributed in Great Britain and Europe by Cassell PLC
Wellington House, 125 Strand, London WC2R OBB, England
Distributed in Australia by Capricorn Link (Australia) Pty Ltd.
P.O. Box 6651, Baulkham Hills, Business Centre, NEW 2153, Australia
Manufactured in the United States of America
All rights reserved

Sterling ISBN 0-8069-9833-4

Contents

1 What to Expect

P eople get interested in weight training for dozens of reasons. Some do it to improve their performance in sports. Others want to feel more fit and be stronger. The vast majority, however, train with weights to look better. They want a shapelier, bigger body, with muscles that can flip from a relaxed state to rock-hard in a fraction of a second. That they feel better and enjoy vigorous good health and strength is merely a pleasant bonus.

Are muscles attractive? You betcha! Of course, as with any sport or hobby, there are those whose fanaticism takes them too far, but, generally speaking, the men and women who train regularly with weights and follow a healthy regimen of sensible eating do develop more attractive bodies. Their muscle bellies enlarge and rise from their skeletal frame with attractive curves, their overall tone increases, and their strength and fitness improve. Heck, statistically, they're even going to live longer.

How long does it take to get results? Actually, you'll notice results the day after your first workout. Your muscles will be sore. However, you probably won't see significant results for five to eight weeks. But after six months of consistent training and proper eating, you could totally transform your physical appearance. If you are thin, you can add mass, widen your shoulders, increase your chest, arm, and leg sizes proportionately, and triple your overall strength.

And will you ever feel great! Over the years I have noticed that virtually everyone who begins weight training in earnest stays with it. It's probably the most satisfying pastime there is.

I know the joys of the elite sports, such as sailing, golf, and tennis. I spent years fishing in remote lakes, scuba diving in the Caribbean, and skiing in Austria, but a satisfying free-weight workout in a friendly gym beats them all. How come? Because you can tailor the resistance used in each exercise to exactly match your strength levels, thus avoiding overexertion, strain, or other injuries—but more importantly, weight training is fun because you are sculpting your own body. Want a greater chest size? Could use a few more cuts (definition)? Want your abs to show? It's all within your

(Far left) IFBB pro Gunther Schlierkamp of Germany.
(Left) The incredible abdominals of Paul Dillett.
(Right) Canada's Joe Spinello.

1

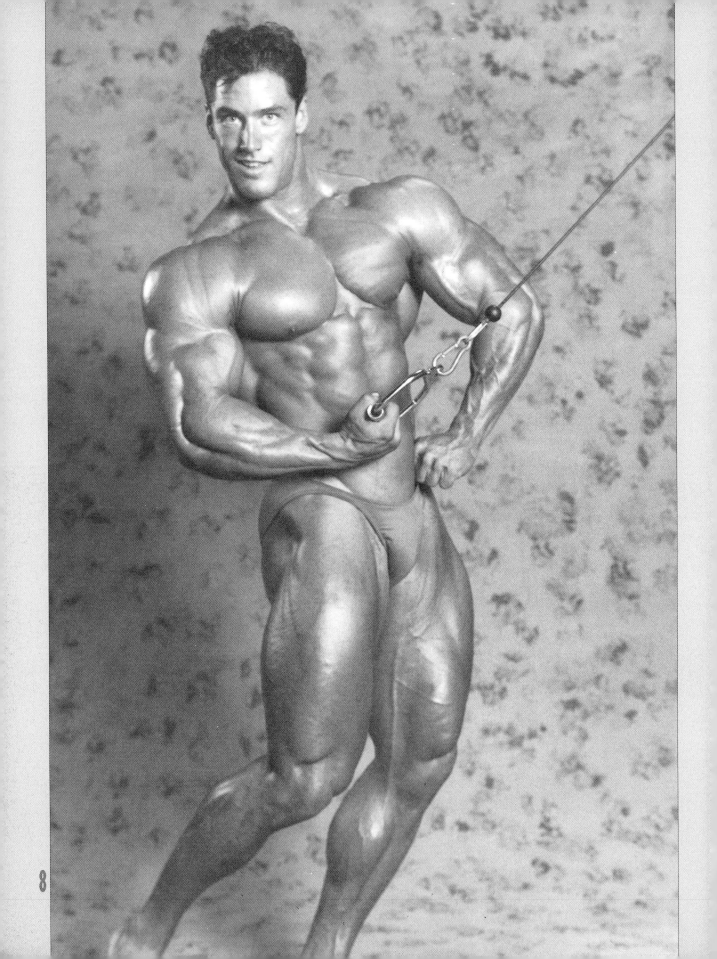

control. What a wonderful sport! I've never regretted one second spent in the gym—and I've been working out for more than 40 years!

If you are already training with weights, then this book will help reinforce the basics of correct exercise procedures, principles, and performance. But for those of you who are complete beginners, I have outlined everything you will need to know to get started with bodybuilding.

Although I have already given you an indication of what kinds of results you can expect, I want to emphasize that you can take your training to almost any level. The pro bodybuilder is the extreme example of what working out with weights can achieve. This book is for the flabby housewife who wants to tone her body, the fitness enthusiast who wants a shapelier physique, and the athlete who needs extra performance strength, as well as for the aspiring bodybuilder who desires added mass. Each can achieve tailor-made results with similar routines that vary only slightly, depending on his or her requirements. So, how are the different levels achieved? It comes down to training intensity, nutrition, and supplementation—all thoroughly discussed in later chapters.

Did I scare you when I suggested that if you start training today, you will stay with it for the rest of your life? Did you feel like you had been given a life sentence? Hey, don't get the wrong idea! You can give up training whenever you want. Nothing bad will happen. If you suddenly stop training, you'll slowly return to how you were before you started working out. If you were previously fat and return to your old eating habits, you will become fat again. Those who were skinny when they began will tend to lose muscle size and gradually become thin once more.

However, based on hundreds of individual observations, my guess is that you will stay with your training. For one thing, it requires hardly any effort to keep in amazing shape. Thirty minutes, two or three times a week, are all it takes to maintain your perfect body.

(Opposite) Dennis Newman is known for his good looks and outstanding proportion.
(Below) Ben Weider and Arnold Schwarzenegger congratulate Michael Francois on his latest win.

2 Sets and Reps

The two basic terms associated with weight training are sets and reps. A rep (short for repetition) is the single count denoting the performance of an exercise. For example, when you push a bar from your chest to arms' length and return the weight to your chest, you have performed one rep. Repeat the procedure 9 times, and you have performed 10 reps. Eight consecutive lifts are known as 8 reps. Get the idea? A set, on the other hand, is the completion of a consecutive number of reps. If you squat with a bar 10 times (10 reps) and then put the weight down for a rest, you will have performed a set. After resting for a minute or two, you may choose to perform another series of 10 reps. This would become your second set. Two sets of 10 reps in bodybuilding language is written 2 x 10; 3 sets of 12 reps is written 3 x 12.

You will notice an increase in muscle mass, strength, tone, and stamina regardless of the number of repetitions you perform; if you follow certain guidelines, you will achieve a greater increase in one aspect than in the others.

Strength

Maximum strength is normally achieved from doing 5 to 8 sets of 3 or 4 reps each set. Occasionally (once or twice a month), athletes will attempt a single set with maximum weight to gauge their progress.

Muscle Mass

Exactly how many reps are needed to stimulate maximum muscle mass has been debated for at least a century, and the number can vary from one individual to another. Also, some have found it beneficial to change the number of reps performed in order to keep their muscles "surprised," or off-guard. For example, working your chest with 4 sets of 10 reps every workout could become boring. Certainly your chest muscles could get used to the same-old, same-old each workout. But what if one day you added considerably more weight and performed sets of 5 repetitions? Believe me, you'd feel it, and the day after your training, your chest muscles would be sore (a sign that they had been

(Right) Gary Strydom of South Africa, now a resident of California.

stimulated more than usual). And what if after a month or two of exercising with 5 reps, you reduced the weight and trained using 12 reps each set? Again, new stimulation (and growth) would be achieved. It pays to change your rep patterns regularly if you are seeking maximum muscle mass. Be aware, however, that the rep range for mass is normally 8–12.

Muscle Tone

Don't need huge mass? Only want to build a toned physique? Try 3 sets of 20 reps. Naturally, you won't be able to use heavy weights following this format, but you will tone your muscles like crazy. Don't bounce or swing the weights when trying to fully tone the muscles. Keep to a moderately constant up-down pace, lowering the weight at the same speed you used to lift it.

Stamina

The sky's the limit when trying to build stamina. It just depends on your fitness target. The average person would be satisfied with the results obtained from doing one set of 50 reps, but there are those who press on into the hundreds. Some men and women choose to use no weights at all when performing high-rep stamina-building exercises. Individuals have been known to perform hundreds, even thousands, of squats, dips, and crunches to maximize their stamina quotient. It all depends on what you want. Check the *Guinness Book of World Records* to see how you rate in the numbers game.

Fitness women Debbie Kruck and Marla Duncan get some sun.

Eddie Robinson of Florida

How Many Sets Should You Perform?

Keep in mind that there is no magic number that works perfectly for everyone. The usual number of sets performed by bodybuilders today is 5. But there are those proponents of "heavy-duty" (all-out-intensity) workouts who only perform 1 or 2 sets for each exercise.

Power trainers interested in maximizing their strength frequently perform a dozen sets of a power lift, but, unlike bodybuilders, they only train using a few select movements.

How does heavy-duty differ from regular training? Normally a set is concluded when you can't manage another complete repetition without an all-out, gut-busting effort. The heavy-duty method would have you go for this last all-out rep, plus perform a couple more "assisted" reps. This is when a training partner applies a light helping hand (or finger) to ease the weight up, so that you can carry on with a couple of repetitions more that you normally wouldn't be able to do unassisted. This high-intensity training is very grueling, and too much of it can cause you to over-train. However, if performed for short periods (three to four weeks), it is one of the key methods for making explosive gains. Heavy-duty training was popularized in the '80s and '90s by Mr. Universe, Mike Mentzer.

Sets and reps constitute the amount of work you assign your muscles. The key is to start light, building up the intensity as you get stronger, but to never work your muscles to the extent that you're unable to fully recuperate before your next workout.

3

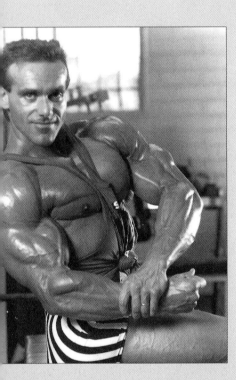

Workout Frequency

How often should you work out? Opinions vary as to which system is best. The advice runs the complete range from training every day to training only one day a week.

Training frequency is tied in with how many body parts you wish to train during your workout. Thirty years ago virtually all bodybuilders trained three days a week. Invariably those days proved to be Mondays, Wednesdays, and Fridays. This choice served a dual purpose. It allowed for a nontraining day between each workout, and it didn't interfere with the weekend. Generally, the Monday, Wednesday, Friday trainer exercised the whole body each training day. This, of course, translates to an individual exercising the entire body three times a week. Today this is considered too much. The modern weight trainer exercises each body part once or twice only per week, which maximizes the chance for fullest recuperation.

There is, of course, some spillover effect from all training. For example, the abs are strongly worked when we perform arm exercises and the back is often trained when we work our legs. However, we do categorize certain exercises as "leg movements" or "arm exercises," because the *primary* muscle action is in the leg or arm area.

These days the tendency is to split up the workout according to body parts. These abbreviated workouts, usually only 40 to 60 minutes long, involve performing several exercises per body part (three to five is typical).

Sometimes workouts are performed on three consecutive days, followed by a rest day, and then on three more consecutive days, followed by another rest day. This translates to training six days a week and resting on one. In bodybuilding terminology, this is known as training three days on, one off.

As you might imagine, there are dozens of permutations. It becomes a matter of selecting a system that fits in with your work and family obligations.

(Far left) John Terilli of Australia. *(Top left)* Vince Taylor.
(Below) Ericca Kern demonstrates that muscles on females can be quite attractive.

Popular choices include, but are certainly not limited to, the following:

One on, one off
Two on, one off
Three on, one off, two on, one off
Three on, one off
Four on, one off
Five on, one off
Five on, two off

If you have any doubts as to which frequency pattern to choose, experiment by trying different systems. Your main consideration should be to adequately stimulate your muscles to bring about the results desired, while making sure that you've allotted adequate rest time to allow for fullest recuperation.

If you haven't fully recuperated, you'll feel tired and have little energy, your interest in training will lag, and your muscles may appear flat and stringy—certainly, a pump will not come easily. On the other hand, if you have recuperated properly, you will have a lot of enthusiasm and your zest for life will be at 110 percent, your muscles will hunger for each successive workout, and you'll get a pump like you wouldn't believe.

Once you have decided on a frequency pattern, you need to slot in your body-part training for each workout. The most common method used today is to train two body parts per workout. But quite often only one body part is trained in each workout on a three day on, one off basis. This translates to each body part being trained once per week. Those with lots of time (many pro-bodybuilders) regularly train twice a day—once in the morning and once in the afternoon—but this is a bit extreme for the average individual. The following is an example of the most commonly used method of training frequency.

Three On, One Off, Two On, One Off

Day One: back and calves
Day Two: quads and hamstrings
Day Three: chest and abs
Day Four: rest
Day Five: shoulders and triceps
Day Six: biceps and traps
Day Seven: rest

Remember that, when it comes to frequency, you can be as creative as you wish—there is nothing written in stone about which methods are most workable. If you would feel more comfortable training your entire body three times a week, you could do so by performing your complete workout every Monday, Wednesday, and Friday. Any choice of days is fine so long as you have at least one day of rest between workouts. You could even split your routine into two equal parts and train half your body at a time, working out six days a week.

(Opposite) John Simmons of Ohio.
(Below) Darin Lannaghan poses before the mirror and for photographer Jason Mathas.

4

Warming Up and Stretching

First the good news: Bodybuilding is a very healthy sport. Weight training is the most perfect form of exercising the body, because, regardless of what shape we're in, we can tailor the barbells and dumbbells to our individual strength levels. Now the bad news: Every serious athlete, including bodybuilders and weight trainers, suffers an occasional injury. It can be something as simple as a weakened wrist or as serious as a severely torn muscle or tendon requiring surgery.

Before you throw this book down in disgust, let me hasten to add that most gym injuries are minor muscle strains or tears caused by poor exercise form and too heavy weights or from failure to adequately warm up. The remedy for such injuries is to rest the injured zone. Do not perform any exercise that will aggravate the condition or is painful to the area.

Severe muscle tears should be iced (ice cubes in a bag, pressed onto the area) and then bandaged, elevated, and rested completely. It's important to consult a doctor at your earliest opportunity. Full recuperation could take weeks if the injury is serious.

Very few people have jobs that require much in the way of physical exercise; most of us sit at a desk. This all changes when we go to the gym to train. Instead of holding a one-ounce pencil, we lift a 100-pound barbell. In place of punching a keyboard, we hammer away at the heavy bag. Our physicality is challenged to the hilt. It is imperative, therefore, that we warm up the body before we struggle to lift even moderate weights. A warm-up increases the blood flow to the muscles, stretches them out, and generally prepares them for maximum exertion. Moreover, warm-ups greatly reduce the chance of injury.

Arnold Schwarzenegger has said that sometimes when he was training for a contest, he'd be so psyched up that he skipped warming up. He'd plunge right into a heavy workout, invariably pulling muscles, and setting himself back a couple of months.

The warm-up takes place at the beginning of each workout and at the start of each new exercise, whatever it is.

(Far left) Amy Fadhli. *(Top left)* Jean Pierre Fux poses during a competition. *(Right)* Matt McGlaughlan drops his track pants for the camera.

Preworkout Warm-up

When you first get out on the gym floor, you may feel sort of lazy. Your muscles may be cold; certainly they will not be pumped (unless you cycled to the gym). Often, the last thing you feel like doing is to train strenuously. Have no fear—after a good warm-up, your heart will be a-pumpin' and blood will be circulatin' like there's no tomorrow. Start with riding a stationary bike for 5 to 10 minutes, or you could jog on the jogging machine (or trot on the spot if there's no jogging apparatus) for a few minutes. Jumping rope is another alternative, although considerably more demanding.

Your goal is to speed up your circulation and resting heart rate. This is not the time to challenge your lung capacity or staying power. You can do a few arm swings to warm up the shoulder joints or a variety of stretches. After this brief warm-up, you'll be ready to rock 'n' roll into the real workout.

Individual Exercise Warm-up

Before starting each exercise, you have to warm up by using light weights for that same exercise. For example, before starting heavy bench presses, warm up by doing 20 to 30 repetitions in the bench press with about half your normal weight. For instance, if you normally curl with 80 pounds, then warm up with 40.

The weight should not be so light that the muscles are barely challenged. You need a significant resistance to properly prepare the muscles for heavier reps. As

(Left) Aaron Baker stretches his legs before training.
(Below) California's beautiful Melissa Coates.

time goes by, you will learn just how much weight to use for each individual exercise warm-up. As a general guide, use approximately half the weight you normally use for 10 reps. Keep in mind that these warm-up repetitions (usually between 15 and 30 reps) do absolutely nothing for muscle development. They are merely your way of saying to your muscles, "I'm giving you some light reps to warm you up. Take your time; fall into it easy. In a couple of minutes, I'm gonna sock it to you hard!"

While we're hovering around the subject of injury, here are a few tips to follow so that you can avoid hurting yourself:

Never accept a challenge from a gym member or a friend to see who can lift the biggest dumbbell or heaviest barbell. Heavy lifting should only be attempted if you have practiced heavy lifting (that is, very low reps with maximum poundage).

Never use maximum effort on a new exercise or even a new bench or machine "angle." For example, if you change your incline bench angle from 30° to 45°, you will be hitting an entirely different "groove" and an injury is not at all unlikely. Work into any new angle or exercise with light reps before going heavy.

Never bounce a weight off your chest when benching, or dip and rebound quickly when squatting. The former can crack the sternum (your central chest bone); the latter can wreck your lower back or knees for a long time. Both are dangerous practices.

Never train in bare feet. A weight dropped on your toes could cause a lifetime of misery. Your gym footwear should give you enough support and grip, yet be pliable enough to allow you to perform full-range calfwork. The big companies like Nike, Brooks, and Reebok offer ideal cross-training and workout shoes at varying price ranges.

Always make sure you are adequately hydrated. Drinking 6 to 10 glasses of water daily is a good practice. A hydrated body helps to eliminate fat and keeps your system working at top capacity. Dehydration, on the other hand, can lead to heat exhaustion and serious illness.

Although you may suffer an injury once in a while, let's hope it's nothing more than a small strain or a bruised ligament. With care, however, you can cruise through your entire lifetime with only the occasional discomfort. Happy squatting!

5

What Makes Muscles Grow?

The answer to this question is both simple and enormously complicated. It's also safe to say that there are many ways to make muscles grow, and the more you utilize all of these applications, the better your chances of reaching your maximum potential.

Scientists have made numerous double-blind experiments in order to discover the secret of muscle growth. Their findings, although documented rigidly and printed out neatly by their sophisticated computers, are virtually useless to the serious hardcore bodybuilder. Scientists are not able to recognize, let alone document, the various intangibles, such as motivation, goal setting, concentration, and outright enthusiasm for obtaining muscle mass. No doubt one day exercise buffs will be able to use science to develop maximum muscle size, but that day is not within sight at current writing. Besides, when did you last see a scientist with 22-inch guns?

During the years I've spent in the sport, I have seen enormous size built by individuals who had no knowledge of physiology, nutrition, or sophisticated training principles. Conversely, I have seen others who devoured every bit of training advice, yet still remained with only moderate development.

So what makes our muscles grow? Here is what we know on the subject.

Increased Intensity

Adding weight to your resistance poundage puts extra stress on the muscles being worked. This will translate to increased strength (if you can manage to achieve your regular rep count), usually followed by an increase in muscle size. But adding weight is not always easy, or even possible. Sometimes an increase in weight resistance is accomplished at the expense of a decrease in good exercise form. Needless to say, this usually (not always) negates the desired purpose of achieving added mass. All things being equal, however, added resistance will bring about more size and strength.

Added Nutrition

When we eat more, we tend to put on weight. The calories can be derived from fat, carbohydrates, or protein, or a combination of all three. Admittedly, not all

(Left) Flex Wheeler. *(Right)* Renel Jan Vier.

individuals will immediately gain size by upping their food intake. Some have high metabolisms and ectomorphic (skinny) body types, which make it difficult to achieve significant gains in weight or muscle mass. Generally, however, increased calories will aid you in your quest for faster gains.

A warning: Should you dramatically increase your food intake, you could find yourself adding more fat than muscle. Eat only enough food to enable your body to utilize it for energy and muscle building. If you eat too much, it will be stored as adipose tissue.

Improved Recuperation

All the training in the world is useless if your muscles are not allowed to fully recuperate after each workout. Bodybuilders need more relaxation, rest, and sleep than other athletes. Try to get a minimum of eight hours' sleep each night and to relax for at least half an hour after each meal. Obviously, a manual job working as a road digger or a sheet-metal worker is not as conducive to muscle recuperation as a vocation as a desk clerk or computer operator.

Most male professional bodybuilders, it may be noted, do not have formal jobs. They try to make ends meet with money they make from guest posing spots, prize money, and product-endorsement contracts. Still, only a few make a satisfactory living from the sport.

Stick-to-itiveness

There is no substitution for regular training. Those on-off trainers never make the big time. You should only miss a workout if you are genuinely sick or extremely tired. Many people give the gym a miss believing they are tired, when in fact they are merely lazy. You must learn to recognize the difference.

There may be times when you have had a hard or stressful day, or you had to work longer hours than usual. Should you work out? Or should you take the day off? The answer is, you work out, but to a lesser extent. Just perform 2 or 3 sets per body part to keep

(Left) Craig Titus (of California), U.S.A. National Champion.
(Below) Montreal's Joe Spinello shows his "heavy" equipment.

the muscles stimulated. On the other hand, if you have a heavy cold, the flu, or a headache, take the day off, because training would likely worsen the situation.

Motivation

Enthusiasm for training and gaining is paramount. If you merely go through the motions when you train, your body will at best hold to the status quo. It will not get stronger or bigger. Keep motivated. Study books, videos, and magazines on bodybuilding. Become an expert on the subject. If bodybuilding is currently your hobby, make it your passion. Rekindle your enthusiasm. Think about what you are training for. To look better to the opposite sex? To succeed in competition? To improve sports performance? Reestablish your needs. Set new goals. Remember, a goal is a dream with a deadline. Visualize how you will look in three months, and go full-steam ahead. As the Nike ad says, Just do it!

Choice of Parents

Okay, so this last aspect is the one thing we can't control, though unfortunately it is the most important. Any man or woman in normal health, tall or short, fat or thin, young or not so young, can benefit from bodybuilding. All can gain muscle and increased strength. The limiting factor is your God-given genetics. Each sport has its own specialized genetic requirements. For example, short men will never make great high jumpers, basketball players, or soccer goalkeepers; tall men can never excel at gymnastics; barrel-chested athletes can never swim with the Olympic team; and world-marathon running champions can't weigh 200 pounds or more.

In the case of bodybuilding, you need to have a certain muscular physical makeup (mesomorphic) to allow you to build maximum muscle mass. This does not mean that skinny or fat people cannot become muscular. We seldom really know how genetically gifted we are until we try our hardest. Most of today's champions were skinny as kids. Their potential was only made obvious after they started regular training.

Do all you can to gain muscle mass. Be sensible, but work hard. Follow the suggestions in this book, and you will change that physique of yours faster than you may have imagined in your wildest dreams.

(Left) Eight-time Mr. Olympia, Atlanta's Lee Haney.
(Right) Ericca Kern on stage at the IFBB Ms. Olympia.

6 The Exercises That Work the Best

Not all exercises work the same for everyone. I have known short men with naturally heavyset, or "genetically gifted," quads who only required the odd set of leg extensions to keep their quads packed from hip to knee with muscle mass to die for. Others (often tall men) would obtain zero development from leg extensions; nothing less than full squats twice a week would do the job. Likewise, I have seen massive calf development on individuals who perform only a couple of sets of seated calf raises, although most bodybuilders have to utilize the standing calf raise to really build their lower legs.

Having ascertained that the same exercise can work differently from one person to another, the exercises that I recommend here are the ones I consider to be the most effective for adding pure mass to each body part *for most people.*

Others' evaluations may differ from my own, and, of course, in some cases, they could be close. I do, however, stand by my convictions, and bear in mind that I have been in contact with literally thousands of individual bodybuilders during my lifetime. As editor-in-chief of *MuscleMag International*, a popular bodybuilding magazine that I started way back in 1974, I have also kept in touch on a daily basis with amateur and professional bodybuilders from around the world, frequently asking them about their training methods and favorite exercises, sets, reps, and so on. Without further rhetoric, then, if you only have time to perform one exercise per body part, these would be my suggestions.

Shoulders (Deltoids)

I would unequivocally choose the *press-behind-neck* (from squat racks or seated pressing bench) as the best single deltoids exercise. The grip or hand placement should be such that when the upper arms are parallel to the floor, the forearms are perpendicular (at right angles) to the (vertical) upper arms.

Secondary exercises that can be performed with the press-behind-neck movement include the seated dumbbell press, the dumbbell lateral raise, and the bent-over flye.

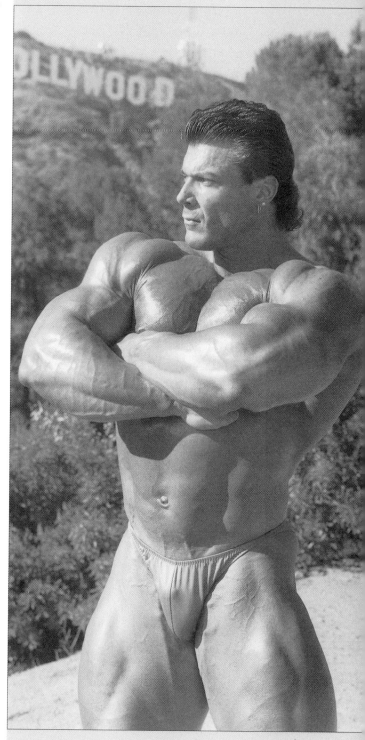

(Left) Perennial Serge Nubret of France.
(Right) Gerard Dente of New Jersey.

(Top left) Ron Coleman uses dumbbell curls for maximum arm development. (Left)California's Tom Platz, the un-crowned Mr. Olympia, works his back with bent-over rows. (Above) Jay Cutler demonstrates that a well-built back looks great from any angle. (Opposite page) New Jersey's Renita Harris displays the type of form built from weight training.

Upper Arms (Biceps)

No doubt in my mind, the *barbell curl* reigns. Grip the bar with a slightly wider than shoulders-width hand spacing, and, without any significant leaning or rocking, raise the bar evenly up and down.

There are literally scores of biceps exercises, but I also rate the incline dumbbell curl (bench set at a 40° angle) and the Scott preacher curl (bench top at 50°) as very highly effective biceps builders.

Upper Arms (Triceps)

It's not easy to figure out the best single triceps exercise. The most popular movement for the area is the pulley machine pressdown. It is a pleasant exercise to perform, works the triceps over a full range of movement, and is definitely a perfect exercise for pumping up these three-headed muscles.

But for sheer mass building, the supine *close-grip bench press* is superior, especially if you want to make a quantum leap in triceps growth. This is a multijoint movement (both the shoulder and the elbow joints are mobilized during the repetitions), as opposed to a unijoint, or isolation, action, which is the case with the triceps push-downs (in which only the elbow joints are mobilized).

Although the close-grip bench press will give you quick triceps size, it will not take your arm development to that outrageous or eye-popping dimension that you see on some advanced bodybuilders. No multijoint (often known as basic) movements will take you to that degree of development. This is where the pumping action of the press-down comes into its own. Curiously though, a unijoint movement alone will not give you huge mass.

Upper Back

In the case of the upper back, there are two completely different aspects of development that have to be considered. Therefore, each has to be allotted a single best exercise.

The first facet is back width. This involves the actual stretching out of the scapulae (shoulder blades) to enhance the all-important V-shape that typifies the bodybuilder's unique appearance. The best exercise to bring about this stretched effect is the *wide-grip chin*. It matters not if the pull-up action is done to the front or the back of the neck. It is important that the elbows are held back (under the bar) throughout the exercise.

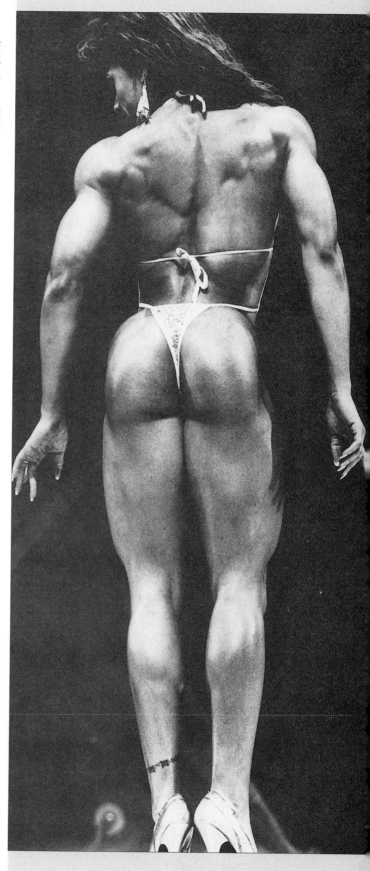

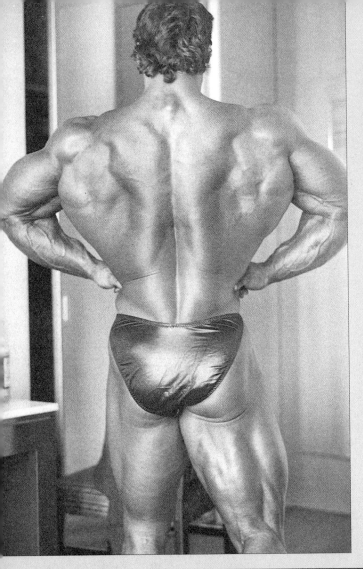

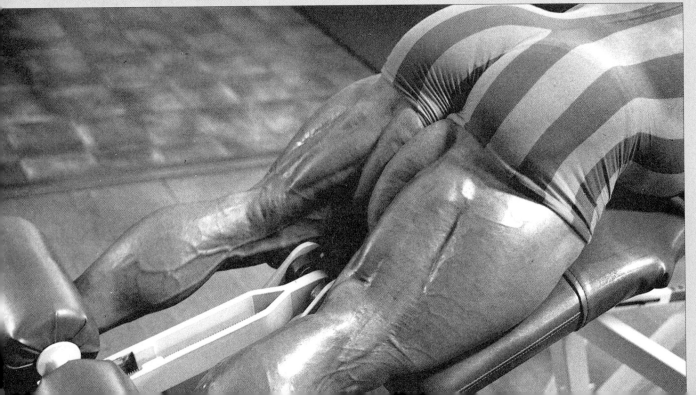

The second aspect of upper-back development is the actual back thickness. The most effective movement for thickness is the *bent-over barbell row*. Beware, however, that if you have any lower-back problems, this exercise could aggravate the condition. Always keep the knees slightly bent and pull the bar up into the waist area, not the chest.

Quads

Love 'em or hate 'em, the best quad (thigh) exercise is the *regular back squat*. Again, this is a multijoint movement (the knee, ankle, and hip joints are all involved), and, as with most basic exercises, marked growth is almost instant. In fact, seasoned bodybuilders who have not squatted in a while know that they can easily add 2 or 3 inches of quad mass with just three or four squatting workouts. Of course, these workouts have to be several days apart (five or six) to allow for growing time, but, believe me, this is not an exaggerated claim.

Leg Hamstrings

There are a variety of specially designed machines for this area. Some involve sitting upright and curling the legs down and towards you. Others involve curling one leg at a time in a standing position. The best exercise, however, is the *lying leg curl* movement using free-weight resistance (as opposed to pulleys, compressors, or pumps). Choose a machine that provides good resistance throughout the movements.

Traps

The fastest traps growth comes from deadlifting. The *deadlift* exercise has to be performed with a flat back and bent knees. Do not confuse this exercise with the stiff-leg deadlift, which is primarily a lower-back and hamstring movement. With the deadlift, you should quickly build up to using heavy weights. In the stiff-leg variety, heavy weights are never used.

A supplementary exercise for the traps is the barbell shrug. It's a good traps movement and one that could be substituted for the deadlift if you find it too physically demanding (or if you have a lower-back problem).

(Top far left) A V-shaped back is what today's bodybuilding is all about—Gerard Dente is the model. *(Top left)* The multiple Ms. Olympia, Lenda Murray. *(Bottom left)* David Palumbo shows us how well-developed hamstrings can accentuate the legs. *(Right)* Ian Harrison of Great Britain.

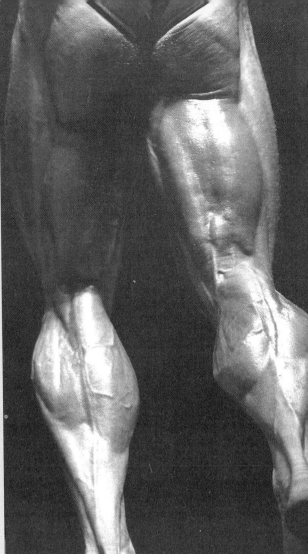

Calves

Nothing beats the *standing calf raise* using a selectorized weight stack. Even beginners will find that the lower legs will quickly gain in strength and development. It is important that the individual rise up as high as possible on the toes and then lower the heel as far as possible when descending for each repetition.

Chest

Still the best overall chest exercise is the *bench press*. Beware of bouncing the weight off the sternum (you could crack it!). Keep elbows back. Upper arms should be in a straight line.

Other worthwhile chest exercises include the incline dumbbell bench press and the incline flye.

(Top far left) Check out Gary Strydom's chest "cuts." *(Top left)* Diamond-shaped calves are the aim of every bodybuilder. *(Bottom left)* Michael Francois. *(Above)* Sweden's Svend Karlsen.

Lower Back

You can't beat the *prone hyperextension* movement for the lower back. The beauty of this exercise, unlike other lower-back movements, is that it is a safe procedure.

Supplementary lower-back exercises include good mornings and stiff-leg deadlifts, but don't handle huge weights. Injury could result.

Abdominals

The most scorching of all ab exercises is the *hanging leg raise*. It is so difficult that when it's performed the midsection is forced to react (and build) quickly. The knees should be bent slightly as the reps are performed. The straight-leg variety, although more difficult, does not involve the abdominal muscles in the same way as when the legs are bent.

Forearms

Most exercises involve the forearms to a certain degree. Certainly whenever we hold a barbell or a dumbbell, the forearms are involved. Consequently many bodybuilders do no specialized forearm exercises at all.

For those whose forearms lack development, it would be a good idea to include some specialized training that attacks the area exclusively. The forearms have two main areas of development, so there is a single best exercise for each area.

The forearm belly (*flexor carpi radialis*) is best worked with the *seated wrist curl* movement using a barbell. The upper-outer reaches of the forearm (*supinator longus*) are best activated by the regular use of the *reverse curl* (remember to use light weights and very little body motion and to keep the wrists straight).

All of the aforementioned exercises and more are explained in detail and pictured in Chapter 9.

Those with limited time can build a very fine physique by only using these best single exercises for each body part. However, the building of a *championship* physique will require the use of these exercises plus supplementary movements to add vital detail and shape. The choice is yours.

(Far left) Check out the arms of California's Aaron Baker. *(Left)* Switzerland's Jean Pierre Fux. *(Right)* Kim Chizevsky.

7
Imagery, Goal Setting, and Motivation

A film executive, after meeting Arnold Schwarzenegger for the first time, remarked to a friend that Arnold's most underappreciated muscle was the one between his ears. Not only did Arnold train hard in his day, but he also applied his mind to its fullest potential to not only improve his training, but also reach specific goals in bodybuilding and later in show business. Like so many athletes, the Austrian Oak knew instinctively that the mind leads us towards success or failure depending on how it's programmed.

Imagery

"Nothing happens unless first a dream," wrote philosopher Carl Sandburg. Take a moment now to dream yourself. What do you want to achieve as far as your health, strength, fitness, and physique are concerned? See in your mind's eye the finished product. You may want to choose a movie star or physical culturist to emulate. Conceive it to believe it. An exact cloning, of course, is impossible, but you can at least try to develop abs like Flex Wheeler's or arms like Eddie Robinson's. Our genetic boundaries may limit us to an extent, perhaps even greatly, but at least we can aim to realize our fullest potential, whatever it is. It all starts with a crystal-clear dream.

Goal Setting

A goal is merely a dream with a deadline. I believe that very little of significance happens to us in our attempt to climb the ladder of success unless we set goals. We all have goals, whether we know it or not, and they have a profound effect on our lives. The secret of success is to unleash your true power by setting goals. Your goals must be reachable and yet exciting enough to inspire you to greatness. Aim to achieve something in three or six months. But be careful not to set wild, impossible long-term goals, because you could become disenchanted with your efforts.

Right now, consciously choose your goals. Do you want to gain 10 pounds of lean muscle in three months? How about aiming to knock off 4 inches from your waistline? What about increasing your bench press to 200 pounds... 4 reps?

(Left) Mauro Sarni of Italy.
(Right) Daniella Morlanne of Miami, Florida.

(Far left) Canada's scintillating Laura Creavalle. *(Left top)* Porter Cottrell flexes during a contest posedown.
(Left bottom) The "glutes" and "hams" of bodybuilder Hamdullah Aykutlu are unbelievable.
(Above) IFBB pro Ron Coleman.

Here are some guidelines for goal setting:

1. Take 10 minutes to come up with a short-term, exciting, workable, achievable goal that would make you happy.

2. Decide to achieve this goal within a set period of time, and then determine how much progress you need to make towards it each week. For example, if you are currently bench-pressing 100 pounds for 10 reps, and your goal is to use 150 pounds for 10 reps within 10 weeks, then you will have to increase your bench press by 5 pounds per week for 10 weeks.

3. Follow up your plan with action. All the goal setting in the world is useless without taking initiative and going the extra mile to actualize your goals. Your bench press will not go up by 5 pounds a week for 10 weeks if you merely go to the gym and train as usual. It will happen only when you persist and settle for nothing less. There are no excuses.

4. Above all, have fun and adopt a confident attitude. Remind yourself at odd times during the day of your goal. Tell yourself that achieving it is a piece of cake. Allow your heart to race at the thought of its completion. Tell yourself that the deadline will be reached—no problem. You can even allow yourself to dream about what your next target might be once this current goal is reached.

Motivation

The secret of unleasing your true power is passion. Many of us have this motivation naturally. Some of us have too much of it. Passion or ambition can so control our lives that we can become consumed with our own importance. Overzealousness can lead to ulcers, illness, and worse.

Most of us, however, lack a clear focus. We are only partially motivated to exceed ourselves. We have wishes and desires, but they need rekindling to maintain their potency. If your motivation is lacking, then keep the fires burning by reading all the bodybuilding and fitness magazines. Read books on the subject, view videos, and attend contests. Motivation has to be stimulated now and again, as every athlete knows. When it's an integral part of your life, you are truly blessed.

(Left) San Diego's Milos Sarcev is known for his perfect proportions. *(Above right)* Lee Apperson, Debbie Kruck, and Marla Duncan. *(Bottom right)* Charles Clairmonte, Lee Labrada, and Mike Francois.

8

Home Versus Gym Training

These days my life is what you might call comfortable, but it wasn't always so. In my teens and early twenties, I couldn't afford membership in a gym nor did I have the money to buy a set of weights for a home-gym setup, let alone to buy benches, lat machines, squat racks, and so forth.

What I did manage to do was set up a steel pipe (bar) in the backyard between two trees. It wasn't exactly horizontal, so in order to equalize my training, I'd perform one set facing north and the next set facing due south. I didn't want unbalanced lat development! As for my weights, these were created from yet another bar with two square biscuit tins. I placed rocks inside the tins and sealed them with poured concrete. I was limited to two bars. One was 115 pounds and the other was 185 pounds. Maybe that's why I became a fairly good curler yet never developed much as a squatter or bench presser. My Mickey Mouse weights didn't allow for any real strength development.

Perhaps some of you less fortunate guys can identify with my lack of finances in my youth. I couldn't afford a set of weights until I was 27 years of age, and a home gym was attainable only after I had reached 30.

Today I have the luxury of having my own home gym and I can train for free at virtually any commercial gym that strikes my fancy. The owners, once they find out I own a bodybuilding magazine, refuse to take my money, even though I offer it. But the irony is, I'd gladly go back to my rock-filled biscuit tins— if I could be 25 again. It was all so much fun.

Which Is Best?

It may not be the eternal question, but the debate rages on: Is it better to train at home or at a gym? The point that begs an answer is, how well equipped is your home gym? If you just have a flat bench and a set of dumbbells, you are not sufficiently equipped to build a superior physique. At the very least, you need barbells, dumbbells, an adjustable flat/incline bench, squat racks, a leg-extension machine, a chinning bar, a lat machine, and a calf-raise unit. Of course, it would also be nice to have a Smith machine, hack-squat apparatus, and a Scott curl bench. But needless to say, however well-equipped your home-gym setup is, it could not compete with the amount or variety of apparatus available in most commercial gyms.

(Left) Alan Ichinose, 1989 Nationals lightweight winner, Miami, Florida.
(Above) Jean Paul Guillaume.

45

Home-Training Advantages

- When you train at home, you don't have to brave inclement weather or traffic jams to work out. Everything is all right there in the comfort of your home.

- You don't have to wait in line to use the squat racks, lat machine, or any other piece of apparatus.

- When you exercise at home, you can take a break from your training (after working a particular body part, for example) any time you want.

- You can play the music you wish to train by, or can exercise in silence. The choice is yours.

- You can shout, curse, yell, growl, and even drop your weights at home. Not so in a commercial gym.

- You don't have to endure the stares of others. Nor will anyone try to engage you in conversation when you are trying to focus on your workout.

- Once home-gym equipment is paid for, it will last forever. At the gym, you have to pay an annual fee.

- Some people prefer to train alone. They have the discipline and prefer to fly solo.

- You can decorate your home gym with posters and pictures that you like.

Advantages of Training in a Commercial Gym

- A commercial gym has a competitive ambiance, which is conducive to making progress.

- Training partners are available in commercial gyms. They can encourage you during the final reps of a set and also help you with forced or assisted reps.

- Commercial gyms afford a huge variety of apparatus. Barbells and dumbbells are prefixed in 5-pound increments, benches in all shapes and sizes abound, and equipment of all kinds is available.

- Commercial gyms allow you to get out of the house, away from whining kids or grumbling spouses. If either is a problem, a big gym can seem like a refuge.

- Commercial gyms are usually air-conditioned. If you don't have an air-conditioned home gym, summer training can be a nightmare.

- New friendships can be formed with people of similar interests.

- Fitness tests are usually available, as are heart-rated machines that are tailor-made to your fitness levels.

- In the milieu of a commercial gym, you'll be kept informed about new trends, exercise tips, and upcoming contests.

So there you go. The choice is yours. In my experience, I've seen many people switch from gym training to home training and just as frequently from home training to gym training. The change seems to be worthwhile in either case. Whatever your decision ... hit the weights regularly!

(Opposite) Mark Stone of New York City. *(Right)* Tom Jimenez looks as impressive as ever in this semi-relaxed pose. *(Below)* Mike Christian poses in Gold's Gym, California.

9

The Exercises

Chest/Pectorals

Bench Press

Start

GOAL: To work the pectoralis major muscle that covers the entire rib cage. The front delts and triceps also receive some work, as do the synergistic muscles, the lats and serratus.

COMMON MISTAKES: Flattening the chest at the top and pushing up with the delts and triceps, instead of the pectorals; lifting the lower back and hips off the bench; bouncing the bar off the chest.

Description:

- Choose a weight that allows between 8 and 12 reps the first working set.

- Lie on the bench press, the weight over your face, not your chest. You need to leave room so that the bar doesn't hit the uprights as you push it overhead.

- Choose a medium-wide grip. For most people, this is shoulders' width to a couple of inches outside the shoulders. Make sure your grip is even so that the bar is properly balanced.

- Before taking the weight off the rack, "preset" your pectoral girdle to facilitate better pectoral isolation by arching your sternum (chest bone) without arching your lower back off the bench. At the same time, feel as though you're pushing your rear delts down and back (towards the glutes). Maintain these vital positions throughout the set. Don't ease up!

- Now you're ready to benchpress, because this puts your pecs in an ideal, strong, biomechanically correct position.

- Lift the bar off the rack, and then lower it slowly and in a controlled manner (do not bounce the bar off your chest) to a point a few inches above the nipple line. Inhale as the bar is lowered to expand your rib cage.

- Exhale as you push the bar up. Try to "think" the action into the pecs. Focus your mind on working the pecs, not the deltoids or triceps.

- Tense the pecs hard at the top, and repeat for the desired number of reps.

TIPS: The bar does not move in a straight up-and-down 90° plane. The exercise plane is tilted. The bar should finish over your eyes at the top, not over your chest.

Finish

49

35° Incline Dumbbell Press

GOAL: To work the upper portion of the pectoralis major muscle, commonly (but improperly) referred to as the "upper pecs."

COMMON MISTAKES: Arching the back and lifting the hips off the bench; flattening the chest at the top and pushing with the triceps and front delts too much.

Start

Finish

Description:

- Clean two moderately heavy dumbbells (ones that allow 8 to 12 repetitions), while lying back on a 30° to 35° incline bench.

- As with the bench press, "preset" your pectoral girdle by arching your rib cage without lifting your back from the bench and pushing the rear delts hard down and back. Now you're ready to press.

- Hold the dumbbells over your face at arms' length with your palms facing each other. This grip allows a fuller range of motion for better stretch.

- Lower the bells slowly in a diagonal down-and-back movement, so that your hands are beside your ears, not your chest. This provides much greater stretch. Try to "feel" the action into the upper pecs.

- Push the bells to an over-the-face position. For more inner pectoral stimulation, turn your elbows in at the top (so that the palms now face your head) and try to make your elbows touch.

Parallel Bar Dips

GOAL: To work the lower and outer sections of the pecs for wide, "flaring" pecs and good pectoral delineation between the abs and lower pecs. The triceps and delts get some work, too.

COMMON MISTAKES: Being too upright and allowing the elbows to drift back, instead of keeping them flared forward, which puts too much emphasis on the triceps; straightening the body, instead of keeping the back hunched.

TIPS: To work your triceps more when dipping (and your pecs less), keep your body upright, and your elbows in tight to the sides and pointing back. Come to full lockout at the top, and lean back to contract your triceps. This builds both the inner and rear heads.

Start

Finish

Description:

- If possible, perform this exercise on V-shaped bars a minimum of 28 to 32 inches apart.

- To work your pectorals, and your triceps less, perform dips in Vince Gironda style: chin on chest; chest concave, with back rounded; feet in front of the body in a "quarter-moon" position.

- Most importantly, the elbows must be spread wide and forward, not in close to the body and back (this involves the triceps too much).

- Lower slowly down and with control, feeling the stretch in the pecs all the way. Really force your elbows to stretch wide and forward (think of trying to touch your elbows in front of your body, a physical impossibility, but it does facilitate the proper movement).

- Push up three-quarters, tensing the pecs hard at the top.

Start

Finish

Triceps

Close-Grip Bench Press

GOAL: To work the long head of the triceps (the part of the triceps that hangs down under the biceps when performing a double-biceps pose), which gives great mass to the triceps. This is a great size builder.

Description:

• Lie back on a bench press, with a medium-heavy barbell on the rack that will allow you to do about 10 to 12 reps. Position your body so that the bar is approximately over your face.

• Choose a narrow overhand grip; anywhere from 6 to 12 inches is suggested. Make sure your grip is even.

• Lift the bar off the rack, and lower it slowly and with control (do not bounce it) to the lower pec line. Your elbows should be close to your body.

• Push the bar upwards and towards your feet, locking out at the top to feel the contraction in your triceps.

• When the reps get difficult at the end of the set, a little bounce is permissible to extend the set and get a couple of extra reps.

Lying Triceps Stretch (or Triceps Extension)

GOAL: To work the outer triceps head, with some long head stimulation. Another excellent mass builder.

NOTE: More emphasis can be placed on different triceps heads by changing the arc that the bar travels. Straight up and down—with the elbows wide, and lowering to the upper chest/neck—works the long head more. Moving the bar in a wide, semicircular arc—with the elbows in and pointing at the ceiling, and lowering the bar to the nose, forehead, or behind the head—works the outer head more.

Start

Finish

Description:

* Lie on a flat bench, your head slightly off to one end, while holding a moderately heavy EZ-curl bar at arms' length over your face. Make sure your grip is even.

* Use a close grip, with your hands about 6 to 8 inches apart. Most find a "thumbless" grip best; the thumb and fingers are on the same side of the bar, instead of wrapped around it.

* Keep your elbows in and pointing straight up at the ceiling at all times. Only your forearms move, not your upper arms.

* Slowly and carefully lower the bar to either your nose or forehead.

* Using triceps power only, push the bar back to your arms' locked-out starting position. Tense the triceps hard, and repeat.

TIPS: For greater range of motion, do this exercise on a 30° decline bench. If your elbows tend to drift forward or sideways, have your training partner hold your elbows and upper arms in the correct position for better triceps isolation.

Standing Barbell Triceps Stretch (or Extension)

GOAL: To work the long head, especially near the elbow and the rear head.

COMMON MISTAKES: Dropping the weight down too fast and trying to rebound out of the bottom, which strains the elbows; not lowering the bar low enough to get a proper stretch in the triceps; allowing the elbows to splay away from the sides of the head, instead of remaining stationary and pointing towards the ceiling.

Start

Finish

Description:

- Use a narrow grip; your hands should be about 6 to 8 inches apart.

- Keep your elbows in tight to your head, the tips of the elbows pointing towards the ceiling at all times. Do not allow your elbows to drift to the sides. Only your forearms move; your upper arms should remain stationary.

- Lower the bar slowly and with control to where it just "kisses" the neck.

- Using triceps power only, return to the overhead starting position. Lock out hard to contract your triceps and repeat.

TIP: If your elbows tend to drift forward or away from your head, have your training partner hold them in place so that they always face towards the ceiling and only your forearms move.

Triceps Pulley Pressdowns (or Pushdowns)

GOAL: To work the various heads of the triceps, especially the outer and medial heads. By starting in an elbows-wide position and pushing straight down to full lockout, the lateral and long heads are targeted and mass is built. By keeping the elbows in to the sides and moving the bar in a semicircular arc to full lockout, the inner and outer heads are targeted and the horseshoe shape is brought out.

COMMON MISTAKES: Pulling the bar down instead of pushing it; using too much weight so that the delts are brought into play to help push the weight down.

TIP: Have your training partner push down on your traps to hold you in place, to get better leverage on the weight

Start

Finish

Description:

- The traditional pressdown is performed with the elbows in tight to the sides, moving the bar in a semicircular arc. Begin by placing your thumb and fingers over the bar— don't wrap your thumb and fingers around it. Try to position the bar across the meaty part of the palms, so that you can *push* the bar down using triceps power, not pull it down using your delts and hands. Make sure your hands are evenly spaced.

- Keep your elbows in tight to your sides. Only your forearms move. Your upper arms do not leave your body. Fight the tendency of your elbows to move away from your body or back, which brings the deltoids into play.

- Make sure your body is a couple of feet from the pulley itself, so that the cable angles away from you. This also gives you room to move the bar over a proper range of motion.

- Moving the bar in a wide, semicircular arc, push it to arms' length using triceps power only. Lock out hard at the bottom.

- Allow only your forearms to return to the starting position at the nipple line of your chest.

TIPS: To give the triceps extra work, push the bar down and slightly away from your body at the bottom. Have your training partner stand behind you and hold your elbows in place, if they tend to drift forward or away from your body.

Version Two

- Use the same grip, with your thumb and fingers draped over the bar. Push the bar down with the meaty part of the palms.

- Stand closer to the bar, slightly bending your upper torso over the bar.

- Spread your elbows out to the sides.

- Push the bar straight down to full lockout. Tense hard at the bottom to contract your triceps, and return to the starting position.

55

Lower Back (or the Spinal Erectors or "Lumbars")

Prone Hyperextension

GOAL: To work the lower-back muscles. The glutes and hamstrings will also come into play. In fact, by positioning your body forward on the bench, you can deliberately target the glutes and hamstrings more if that is your desire.

COMMON MISTAKES: Coming up too high and hyperextending the lower back; not maintaining an arch in the lower back.

Start

Finish

Description:

- Carefully position your body facedown on the hyperextension bench. Lock your feet into the rear foot supports, and place your upper thighs below the crotch across the pad (be careful not to pinch the "family jewels" if you're male!).

- You should be in a comfortable position before you begin. The upper torso should be free to move back and forth in a reverse situp movement.

- Cross your hands across your chest. Bend your torso forward and down with control as far as possible, while maintaining an arch in your lower back (do not let the lower back round). Always maintain the arch throughout the entire range of motion.

- Using lower-back strength only, raise your torso to an angle so that you are about a foot from being parallel to the floor. Do not try to rise up any further than this, as it can cause impingement and stress the spine too much.

- Repeat for the desired number of reps.

TIPS: Placing the hands behind the head changes the stress on the lower back. A barbell plate can be held across the chest for more resistance as you gain strength.

Start

Good Mornings

GOAL: To work the lower-back muscles, although the glutes and hamstrings get some work too.

NOTE: The lower back is very vulnerable to injury, so always use precaution on any lower-back exercise. I suggest you use moderate weights and perform higher reps—12 to 15 per set.

COMMON MISTAKE: Using too much weight, allowing the back to round over at the bottom of the movement.

Description:

- Begin with a moderately light barbell across the back of your shoulders or your upper traps; do not place the bar on your neck. Wrap a towel around the bar to pad it. Make sure the bar is centered across and balanced before beginning. Keep your knees partially locked, heels about 6 to 10 inches apart.

- As with hyperextensions, always maintain an arch in your lower back. Do not allow your back to round. Keep it flat.

- Slowly, and with control, bend forward at your waist until your torso is almost parallel to the floor. Keep your head high and maintain the lower-back arch.

- Using lower-back strength only, return to the starting position.

Finish

Start

Finish

Stiff-Leg Deadlift

GOAL: To work the spinal erectors of the lower back, or to work the hamstrings and glutes. As you will discover, many exercises have a dual purpose. The stiff-leg deadlift is such an exercise. It can be performed on both leg and back days.

COMMON MISTAKES: Dropping the weight down too fast and rebounding out of the bottom. Always perform this exercise smoothly and with deliberate control.

Description:

- To work your lower back, stand on a low, flat bench or a foot-high block of some kind. If using a block, make sure it's solid and secure, not wobbly.
- Hold a medium-heavy barbell at arms' length. As always, make sure your grip is even before beginning.
- Slowly, smoothly, and with control, reach down and try to touch your toes with the barbell. If you're very flexible, try to go beyond your toes, but don't force it if your back is tight or prone to injury. Use caution.
- Using lower-back strength, return to the standing starting position. Repeat for the desired number of reps.

To Work the Hamstrings and Glutes

COMMON MISTAKES: Allowing the lower back to round over instead of maintaining an arch; dropping the weight down too fast and rebounding out of the bottom; coming all the way up to full lockout.

Description:

- To work your hamstrings and glutes, it isn't necessary to stand on a bench or block—you can perform the exercise standing on the floor. Use a narrow stance, heels no more than 6 inches apart.
- Hold a moderately heavy barbell at arms' length.
- While maintaining an arch in your lower back at all times, slowly bend over at your waist as far as possible. Do not allow your lower back to round over at any time. The back is flat. The more you arch, the stronger the stretch on your hamstrings and glutes.
- Lower the bar as far as possible. For most, the bar should stop about midcalf, depending on their flexibility.
- Really try to feel the stretch and pull in your hamstrings. It helps if you push the bar down and slightly away from your body at the bottom. When you have pushed the bar as low as you can—and you should feel a tremendous pull in your hamstrings at this point—pause for a couple of seconds and then see if you can ease the bar an inch or two lower. Now begin your ascent.
- While maintaining tension in your hamstrings at all times, come up two-thirds, pause to tense, and repeat.

NOTE: If you allow your back to round, you'll lose the stretch in your hamstrings. This tends to happen at the bottom, because the natural inclination is to focus on lowering the bar rather than on stretching the hamstrings. If the stretch suddenly lessens, and the bar descends further, you know you've allowed your lower back to round over.

Shoulders (or Deltoids)

Upright Rows

GOAL: To work the front and lateral heads of the deltoids, and the delt-trap tie-ins.

NOTE: This is another exercise that can be performed in two ways to target different muscles.

COMMON MISTAKE: Using too much speed and momentum to heave the bar to the top position, which brings the traps into play too much. This exercise then becomes more of a weight lifter's "high pull" than a bodybuilder's upright row.

Description:

- Hold a moderately heavy barbell in front of your body at arms' length using a close (6 to 8-inch) overhand grip. Make sure your hands are evenly spaced for balance.

- Stand with your feet about shoulders' width apart. Keep your torso upright.

- Pull the bar to approximately nose height. Tense your deltoids, and lower.

- The more you heave the bar up, the more involvement of the traps.

Start

Finish

Wide-Grip Version

NOTE: Special care must be taken with this version because of possible impingement of the deltoids and shoulder injury. When performed properly, it isolates the side or medial deltoid, especially in the hard-to-isolate lower region.

Description:

- Stand holding a moderately heavy barbell at arms' length. Use a shoulders'-width stance for proper balance.

- Take a shoulders'-width grip on the bar. Use a lighter weight than with the narrow-grip version.

- Without any heavy shrugging or heaving of your traps, move the bar straight up and down in a pistonlike motion to under your chin. Use a full range of motion, allowing your arms to straighten at the bottom. Start the upright pull smoothly and slowly. Try to use your deltoids only.

- Try to keep your elbows high and to the sides at all times.

59

Press-Behind-Neck

GOAL: To work the front and side heads of the deltoids. The traps and triceps will get some work too. This exercise can be performed standing or seated at a behind-neck bench. It can also be performed with a barbell or using a Smith machine.

COMMON MISTAKES: Dropping the bar and rebounding off the neck; with the standing version, arching the lower back and kicking with the knees to drive the bar past the sticking point; using too narrow a grip, which impinges the shoulders and brings the triceps into play too much.

Description:

- Take a moderately wide grip on the bar; a couple of inches outside your shoulders is about right.
- To perform the standing version, power-clean the bar to your shoulders, or take the bar off some squat racks or a power rack. Perform the first rep by pressing from the front. Once the bar is overhead, perform the remaining reps by lowering the bar to the base of your neck. Do not bounce the bar at the bottom, or you may injure your spinal column.

Start

Finish

- To perform the seated version, sit at a behind-neck bench with uprights to hold the bar overhead. Take a slightly wider than shoulders'-width grip on the bar.
- Make sure your grip is even so that the bar is balanced.
- Start with the bar from the overhead position. Arch your chest and drop your rear delts before beginning.
- Lower the bar slowly and with control. The bar should just touch the base of your neck before you push it upwards. Never bounce the bar off your neck.
- Inhale as you lower the bar; exhale as you press the bar up.
- Push the bar in a straight line.
- Some bodybuilders like to stop 2 inches from lockout so as to better keep constant tension on the deltoids. Others prefer to lock out hard at the top and to tense and squeeze the delts. Try both ways to see which works and isolates your deltoids best for you.

Seated Dumbbell Press

GOAL: To work the front and side deltoids. The traps and triceps receive work too.

NOTE: Most people prefer to do this exercise seated for better deltoid isolation. Sit at a seated preacher bench turned backwards so that the slanted edge of the preacher hits you across the middle of your lower back. This provides extra support. A regular flat bench will do if a preacher is unavailable.

There are also many versions of this exercise: pressing the palms facing forward at all times (as if pressing a barbell), pressing the palms facing towards the ears at all times, and pressing with a rotating or twisting wrist action. The bells can also be pressed simultaneously, in an alternate seesaw action or one at a time.

COMMON MISTAKES: Leaning back too much and not pulling the elbows back in line with the shoulders; pressing lopsided because one arm is weaker than the other.

Finish

Start

Description:

- Clean two moderately heavy dumbbells to your shoulders, and sit down on the bench.

- Start with your palms facing your ears. Pull your elbows back in line with your shoulders, so that your hands are behind your ears. After you've pushed the bells up to about the top of your head, begin to rotate your wrists so that your palms will face forward at the top.

- Push up until your arms almost straighten.

- Reverse and slowly return to the starting position. Make sure your hands are pulled back in line with your shoulders again. Don't let them get ahead of your body.

- As with the behind-neck press, with this exercise some people prefer locking out at the top and others prefer stopping an inch or two from lockout. It's a matter of personal preference. Try both to see which works best.

Dumbbell Side Laterals (or Side Raises)

GOAL: To isolate and develop the side or medial head of the deltoids.

NOTE: There are more key exercise performance points for performing laterals properly than almost any other upper-body exercise. Pay attention to all suggestions, and try to use extra strict form until you learn the movement.

COMMON MISTAKES: Standing too upright or even leaning backwards during the exercise; raising the wrists higher than the elbows; raising the thumb higher than the little finger; raising the delts and traps instead of the arms; throwing the bells up and allowing them to drop down without resisting the weight.

Description:

- Hold two moderately light dumbbells in front of your body at about crotch level. Use sponges, gloves, or straps to help maintain your grip. Hold your elbows wide apart and to the front of your body. Keep your elbows bent almost at right angles, but the dumbbells themselves should be touching.

- Stand with your feet about shoulders'- width apart. If possible watch yourself in a mirror to monitor your form.

- Lean slightly forward at the hips; about 10 to 15° to begin with. Larry Scott likes to see his rear delt in the mirror as he begins his laterals. He says if you can't see the rear delt, you're too upright. Keep your knees flexed, not straight, and your head up.

- Hold the bells slightly off-center, with your little fingers pressed firmly against the outside plates. The reason for the off-center grip is to better facilitate the so-called "pouring coke bottles" action, in which the little fingers are high and the thumbs are down at the top, to better isolate the deltoid side head. If the thumb is raised higher than the little finger—a classic beginner's mistake—most of the action takes place on the front head, and the side-head isolation is lost. With the off-center grip, gravity tilts the bell for you, so that you don't consciously have to twist your hands.

It also prevents you from overtwisting your hands, which can cause impingement and possible injury.

- Your elbows must be back in line with your shoulders, whereas your hands are in front of your body in a "swan-dive" position.

- With a little kick at the bottom, raise the dumbbells to about ear level.

- Remember to allow your wrists to turn, as if pouring from a bottle. You want the little finger higher than the thumb in the top position.

- Lower the dumbbells more slowly and with control to get the benefit of negative resistance. Don't just drop the bells down. Fight the weights all the way.

- A tip to help with side-head isolation is to always try to keep your elbows higher than your wrists. Raise the weight with your elbows, and let your hands go along for the ride.

- Always try to keep the palms of your hands and the undersides of your forearms facing the ground.

- As the set ends and the reps get harder, it is perfectly all right to start laterals with a kick or a swing of the legs and upper body, because the deltoids don't begin to work until you're almost halfway up. The kicking allows you to extend the set and increase intensity. Just make sure that at least the first 6 reps are 90 to 95 percent strict.

Finish

Bent-over Dumbbell Laterals

GOAL: To work the posterior, or rear, deltoid head.

COMMON MISTAKES: Using too much weight, causing cheating; allowing the upper body to bob up and down; heaving and throwing the weights so that the traps and rhomboids take over.

Description:

- Sit at the end of a flat bench, with your knees and feet together.
- Bend over at the hips, so that your chest is almost pressed against your thighs.
- Extend your legs and hold the dumbbells under your calves to start.
- Use the same "swan-dive" position as you did with the side laterals: elbows back in line with shoulders and bent to almost right angles, and hands in front of the body.
- Also use the same off-center grip to better facilitate the desired "pouring bottle" action.
- Raise your elbows higher than your wrists, and extend your arms to the sides. The bells should be at shoulder level.
- Use a smooth, controlled movement. If you throw or heave the bells up, the traps and rhomboids take over and the rear delts get no work.
- Some bodybuilders prefer using a parallel grip, palms facing each other. Begin with your elbows bent at almost a right angle. Then raise your elbows as high as possible, using rear-delt action only. Lower slowly and repeat.

Start

Finish

Forearms

Reverse Barbell Curls

GOAL: To work the extensors, or top of the forearms. Expect your grip to get work too, and also your lower biceps and brachialis.

COMMON MISTAKE: Using too much weight and throwing or cleaning the weight up, instead of curling it using forearm power.

Description:

* As the name implies, the reverse curl is the reverse of a standard barbell curl. Most bodybuilders prefer to use an EZ-curl bar, because it is easier on the wrists. Hold the bar where the bends are located with a palms-down grip.

* If using a straight barbell, hold the bar in an overhand grip (palms facing down), with your hands slightly wider than a shoulders' width apart. A wider grip eases tension on the wrist; a narrower grip causes wrist impingement and may lead to injury.

* Stand with your feet about shoulders'-width apart, the bar at arms' length in front of your body. Keep your elbows fairly tight to your body. Some people like to rest their elbows on their hip bones for a fulcrum for less cheating.

* Curl the bar back up, using forearm power only. Keep your wrists straight. Do not let them bend towards your body or away from it. This places undue stress on the tendons.

* Repeat for the desired number of reps.

Finish

Start

TIPS: If your hand grip slips, wear gloves or use sponges or straps. Larry Scott found he wasn't able to use as much weight as he wanted on the regular reverse curl, so he came up with a reverse preacher curl that blasts the brachialis and the tops of the forearms. The trick, as with the heavy wrist curl, is to do only the middle three-fifths of the movement. Use a heavy EZ-curl bar, and rest your elbows at the top of the preacher bench, so that they act like a fulcrum from which to pivot. Lower the bar down about one-third from the full extension. Raise the bar up until your forearms are almost horizontal to the floor. Use about 20 to 30 percent more weight than you would for the regular reverse curl, and perform the exercise with a rocking action. A good superset is to perform Scott partial reverse curls with regular reverse curls. Have two bars preloaded, so that there is no undue rest between exercises. Do 3 to 4 supersets for a great forearm pump!

Seated Wrist Curls

GOAL: To work the flexors, or underside of the forearm. The wrists and fingers are strongly stimulated too.

NOTE: The forearms are primarily composed of red "slow-twitch" muscle fiber, like the calves. This means it takes higher repetitions to fatigue and work the muscles of the forearms properly. A minimum of 12 reps per set is suggested, with most sets performed in the 15- to 25-rep range.

There are several ways to perform this exercise: (1) seated, with the tops of the forearms resting across the thighs and the wrists hanging over the knees; (2) seated, with the forearms resting along a flat bench and the wrists hanging over the well-padded end; (3) squatting down low, with the tops of the forearms resting on the thighs and the wrists hanging over the knees; and (4) squatting down behind a 12" x 12" well-padded bench, with the backs of the forearms on the bench and the wrists hanging over the edge. The latter two versions allow you to get under the weight for better leverage, because the knees and hips are lower than the wrists.

COMMON MISTAKE: Doing the reps too fast and losing control of the bar. Do each rep with control and concentration.

Description:
- Assume one of the four positions, as described above. Whichever one you use, your hands must be free and down over your knees or the bench. Your wrist line becomes the focal point on which the barbell balances across your knees or the end of the bench.

Finish

Start

- Hold a moderately heavy barbell in your hands, using a "thumbless" grip—your thumb and fingers are on the same side of the barbell. Space your hands about 10 inches to a foot apart.

- Moving your wrists only, allow them to extend as far down as possible. Then using wrist-forearm power, "curl" the bar back up, raising it as high as you can.

- Do the reps smoothly and with concentration. Stay in control and don't bounce the weight.

- Some bodybuilders, like Dave Draper and Arnold Schwarzenegger, let the bar "roll down" their fingers before curling the weight back up. In this case, allow the fingers to initiate the movement at the bottom, the wrists to finish it at the top. Try it both ways, and see which you prefer.

TIPS: Larry Scott likes to do his wrist curls in a heavy-light fashion, using the 12" x 12" forearm bench. He uses two barbells during one set (having two preloaded barbells saves time by not having to change weights). The heavy one weighs 225 to 250 pounds and is used for 10 reps. The key is, Larry does only partial wrist curls with this huge weight, the middle three-fifths. The wrists bend just a bit and go just a little beyond parallel. When failure comes, he immediately drops the heavy weight and picks up a lighter barbell, weighing 100 pounds, and does 10 full repetitions. That constitutes one set, and he repeats this five times. Give heavy-light wrist curls Larry Scott style a try!

Bicips

Start

Barbell Curls

GOAL: To work the large belly of the biceps for increased biceps mass. The grip and forearms get extra work too.

COMMON MISTAKES: Raising the bar up by shrugging with the traps; bending the lower back and throwing the bar up; allowing the elbows to splay out from the body; allowing the elbows to go back.

Description:

- Begin by holding a moderately heavy barbell at arms' length straight down, with a regular palms-up grip to prestretch your biceps. Stand with your feet about shoulders'-width apart.

- Your upper torso should be upright. To achieve this, arch your chest, keep your back straight, and drop your rear delts down and back. (To get an idea of how important it is to keep the traps and delts out of the curling motion, hold a barbell at arm's length and down and then shrug your delts as high as possible and hold. Now try to curl. You'll find it's impossible to lower the bar or perform a proper curl.)

- The grip width should be wider than your shoulders; your arms should be tight to the sides of your body, with your elbows in and almost resting on your hip bones.

- Hold the bar with a "thumbless" grip; your thumb should be under the bar and on the same side of the bar as your fingers, not wrapped around the bar. Keep your palms parallel to the floor. Work your palms under the bar, while working your elbows into your sides. Your hands should be wide apart, your elbows in. The more you work your palms under the bar, the more your elbows point down as you curl the bar up.

- Lock your wrists. Your wrists should not bend towards your body. This is important for proper biceps contraction. At the top, it's your contracted biceps that stop the bar from hitting your shoulders. If the bar can touch your shoulders, you've bent your wrists and taken tension off your biceps.

- Now you're ready to curl. In a proper strict curl, only the forearms move. The upper arms do not move away from the sides—backwards or forwards. Curl the bar smoothly up, using biceps power until your biceps fully contract. For most people, this is at a 10 o'clock position—not 12 o'clock, as so many believe. The only way the hands can get to 12 o'clock is by raising the elbows and moving the upper arms, which is loose form.

- Your elbows should point down at the top position, not back or to the sides.

- At the top, pause to tense your biceps before lowering the bar.

- Don't just drop the bar from the top position. Lower it slowly and with control to benefit from negative resistance. Fight gravity all the way down.

TIPS: If you find your elbows spreading away from your sides, or the front delts coming forward, or you're having to lean back and kick with your legs to drive the bar past the sticking point, you're using too much weight for proper form. Use a very wide grip to work the inner lower section of your biceps, and a close grip to work the outer section. To prevent cheating for better biceps isolation, either wear a Weider "arm blaster" to keep your elbows stationary, do your curls leaning against a wall so that your elbows can't move back, or have your training partner stand behind you and hold your elbows in place.

Finish

Incline Dumbbell Curls

GOAL: To stretch the biceps and to work the belly of the biceps and some lower biceps too.

COMMON MISTAKES: Lifting the dumbbells with the deltoids and traps, because the bells are too heavy; splaying or spreading the elbows away from the body, instead of keeping them tucked in, also because the bells are too heavy; allowing the hands to turn in at the top, instead of turning them out so that the palms are parallel to the floor and the little fingers are higher than the thumbs in the fully contracted position.

Description:

- Sit on an incline bench at a 45° angle.

- Place the incline bench in front of a dumbbell rack, a bar in a power rack, or a Smith machine set about 2 feet off the ground. When you lay back on the bench, elevate your feet on the bar or rack. This provides better biceps isolation and more stability to the movement. It also allows you to push off with your legs, giving your arms more thrust.

- As you did with the barbell curl, use a "thumbless" grip. Keep your thumb turned out and your palms parallel to the floor. Try to hold the bells mostly in your palms, not your fingers. Try to work your palms down and under the dumbbell handle, so that your elbows point down, not back or away from your body. Again, you are trying to attain a position with your hands wide apart and your elbows in tight to your body.

Finish

Start

- Hold the bells a little off-center, with your little fingers pressed firmly against the inside plates (the opposite of laterals, so that the bells tilt out, not in). This helps you supinate your hands at the top for better biceps contraction.

- Lock your wrists straight—do not let them bend.

- Arch your chest, and drop your rear delts down.

- Start with the dumbbells hanging down and behind your body to prestretch your biceps.

- Try to keep your elbows pointing down as you curl, so that you have a feeling of being under the weight. Don't let your delts move forward or your elbows move away from your body, or you'll bring your front deltoid into play.

- Curl the bells up together smoothly but explosively—that is, build up speed until you reach the top position. Do not swing or throw the bells up.

- As the bells reach halfway, your palms and the undersides of your forearms should face up. At the top, turn your wrists out, so that the little fingers are higher than the thumbs, to supinate the biceps. Do not let the wrists turn in.

- Return the bells to the starting position using control, to get the benefit of negative resistance. Feel the stretch in your biceps, as you move the dumbbells down and back and behind your body to the starting position.

TIP: If you find it difficult to get the proper action on this exercise, have your training partner stand behind you and hold your elbows so that they can't drift back or away from your body.

67

Barbell Preacher Curls

GOAL: To work and isolate the lower biceps.

COMMON MISTAKES: Placing the elbows too low on the slanted preacher bench; dropping the weight to rebound out of the bottom; allowing the arms to completely straighten at the bottom (stop one inch from completely straight).

NOTE: Barbell preacher curls are also known as Scott curls, after the man who made them famous, Larry Scott.

Description:

- Grips of different widths can be employed to attack various muscle fibers of the biceps. The best version is the one used by Larry Scott. Sit at a preacher bench, with your hands wider than your shoulders, and with your elbows in close and just a few inches apart. Position your elbows high on the slant pad. As you sit at the bench, you have to work your elbows in close and force your hands wide apart.

- Hold the bar in a "thumbless" grip, your thumbs on the same side of the bar as your fingers. Keep your thumbs pointing to the sides, in a "hitchhiker" position, and your palms parallel to the floor. Work your palms down and under the bar. The undersides of your forearms should face up at all times.

- As you begin to curl, use some wrist strength to get the bar moving. Once you've moved the weight the first couple of inches, curl with pure biceps power.

- As you curl the bar up, have the feeling that you're trying to pull your elbows together and make them touch. This is a physical impossibility, but it's a good thought to promote the movement with your elbows in and your hands wide apart.

- Remember to keep your wrists locked for proper biceps contraction.

- At the top, pause to tense and squeeze your biceps.

- Lower the bar slowly and with control, to get the benefit of negative resistance, feeling the stretch in your biceps. Don't bounce the bar off the pad at the bottom, as this places great stress on the tendons and connective tissue, and could leave you open to injury.

Start

Finish

Dumbbell Concentration Curls

GOAL: To develop the peak of the biceps by developing the outside head.

NOTE: You can do concentration curls seated, resting the elbow of the working arm on the inside of your thigh, or do them freestanding. The freestanding version, favored by Arnold Schwarzenegger, is described here.

COMMON MISTAKES: Throwing the weight up instead of curling it with biceps power only, because the weight is too heavy (this is a very strict isolation movement—stress form over weight); moving the upper part of the working arm; curling the dumbbell up and into the body, instead of up and away from the body (that is, letting the wrist turn in—with the thumb higher than the little finger—instead of turning it out, so that the little finger is higher than the thumb).

Start

Description:

- While holding a moderately heavy dumbbell, bend over at the waist until your torso is a little above parallel to the floor. If you're holding the dumbbell in your right hand, brace your left hand against your left knee. Have your feet comfortably apart, about at shoulders' width.

- Begin with your right arm hanging at full length in front of your right foot—or even a few inches to the right of it—so that the biceps are completely stretched. Turn your hand so that the palm faces towards your body (knuckles point away), and reach to the right until you feel a strong pull on your biceps. This is your starting position. This little hand twist increases your range of motion and gives your biceps a better prestretch. The stronger the stretch on your biceps at the beginning, the harder they can contract at the top. Many beginners fail to get enough stretch at the bottom.

- Hold the bell mostly in your palm, not your fingers. Work your palm down and under the bar, your thumb pointing out to the side, so that your palm is parallel to the floor as the bell comes up.

- As you begin to curl the dumbbell up, turn your wrist out so that your palm and the underside of your forearm now face up. Remember, only the forearm moves; the upper arm stays stationary.

- Lock your wrists, as you would on any curling exercise.

- The dumbbell is curled across and away from your body. Many people think you curl the dumbbell in your right hand across your body until the hand turns in and it hits the left deltoid. It doesn't. The right hand turns out so that the little finger is higher than the thumb, which supinates the wrist for extra biceps contraction.

- The bell should be a foot or so away from the left delt and under the face.

- At the top, pause to tense and squeeze the biceps hard for a count of two. Then slowly return to the starting position, rotating your wrist at the bottom so that the back of your hand faces away from your body.

- As the name implies, use deep concentration.

- Alternate arms.

- You'll know you're doing the exercise correctly if you get a good cramping feeling in your biceps.

Finish

Quads

Back Squats

GOAL: To work the frontal thighs for mass and the outer thighs for sweep, and to develop power in the thighs, hips, and glutes.

NOTE: The closer the stance, and the higher you place the bar on your shoulders, the more tension you can place on your thighs and less on your glutes and hips. Always squat using squat racks, the racks of a power rack, or a Smith machine.

COMMON MISTAKES: Bending forward too much when descending and rocking back and forth when ascending, which is very stressful to the lower back; ducking the head down and coming up glutes first, instead of using thigh power to ascend with the hips forward and the glutes down and low; allowing the lower back to bend and round over; bouncing out of the bottom to gain momentum to drive past the sticking point; not descending low enough; allowing the knees to spread apart when ascending.

Description:
- Elevate your heels on a 2-inch block if you have trouble keeping your balance.
- Keep your feet 6 inches to a foot apart.
- Keep the bar high on your traps to better facilitate keeping an upright torso.
- Wear a weight belt for better lower-back protection. Once you've taken the bar from the racks, center the bar on your shoulders/traps so that it's balanced properly, lean forward about 10° at the hips, and arch your lower back and keep your back flat, not humped.
- Once you're ready to squat, lock your lower back into one position and maintain it throughout the set. Never allow your lower back to round over. Keep your head up and look ahead.
- Arch your chest, take a deep breath, and descend slowly to a point an inch below parallel to the floor. Keep your abs and upper body tight. Feel as though you're coiling your body like a spring. Pause (never bounce out of the bottom, as this puts too much strain on the knees) and then explode up, until you're at the standing starting position again. Your lower back should still be arched, and you should be leaning slightly forward. Repeat for the desired number of reps.

TIPS: To work the outer sweep more, push from the heels as you ascend. To work the middle quad more, push from the balls of the feet.

Start

Finish

Hack Slide

GOAL: To work the lower thigh around the knee. The outer, middle thigh also receives some stimulation.

COMMON MISTAKES: Descending too fast and rebounding out of the bottom, which is dangerous to the knees; failing to go low enough for fear of not being able to get back up.

NOTE: To work the outer-thigh sweep, place your feet high and wide on the foot platform and push off hard from your heels. To work the lower thighs, place your feet low on the foot platform, heels close together, and push off from the balls of your feet. To work the middle quads, place your feet in the middle of the platform, about a shoulders' width apart, pushing from the balls. You can also place the heels together in a V-shape and low on the platform, to work the "teardrop" muscle above the knee.

Description:

- Get into position on the hack-slide machine. Assume your chosen stance, grip the handles to free the slide, and descend slowly and with control to a point well below parallel to the floor.
- Push up hard and stop one to 2 inches from lockout, to keep constant tension on your thighs. Pause to tense and squeeze your thighs.
- Lower and repeat for the desired number of reps.

Start

Finish

71

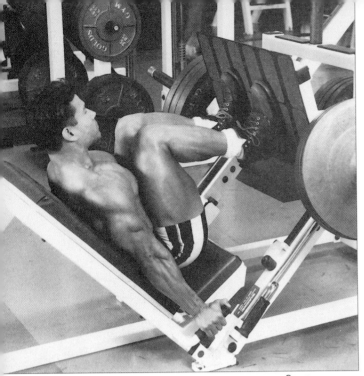
Start

45° Leg Press

GOAL: To work various aspects of the quads and hamstrings.

COMMON MISTAKES: Dropping the weight too fast to rebound out of the bottom; not setting the back support properly, so that too much stress is placed on the lower back; not lowering the weight far enough (partial-only reps).

NOTE: As with the hack squat, different parts of the thighs can be worked, depending on where the feet are placed on the foot platform and from which part of the foot you push off. For example, if you place your feet high at the top of the foot platform, so that your heels are on the top edge and your toes are off the platform completely, you can actually target the hamstrings quite strongly. Use a wider than shoulders'-width stance for this version. Conversely, if you place your feet at the bottom of the foot platform, so that your toes are on the bottom edge and your heels are off completely, you can work the lower thighs strongly around the knees. Use a narrow stance—from heels touching to no more than a foot apart. To work the outer thighs for mass and sweep, place your feet in the middle of the platform but wide apart. Push off from the heels. To work the middle of the quads, place your feet in the middle of the platform, close together, and push from the balls of your feet.

Description:
- Decide on the amount of weight you wish to use and the aspect of the thighs you wish to work. Set your feet accordingly.
- Lower the weight slowly and with control, coiling your legs like a spring.
- Allow your knees to hit your chest or your armpits, depending on which version you are doing.
- Explode up vigorously. Stop one inch from full lockout (always maintain a little bend in your knees), and pause to tense and squeeze your thighs.
- Lower and repeat.

Finish

Start

Finish

Leg Extension

GOAL: To shape and define the quadriceps, to bring out thigh separation and definition, and to develop the "teardrop" muscle above the knee.

COMMON MISTAKES: Swinging the weight up and dropping it down without any resistance.

Description:

- Choose a moderate weight that allows about 15 reps. This is not a low-rep power movement. Very low reps with huge weights could cause knee injury.
- Sit at the leg-extension machine, your ankles under the foot pads. Hold the sides of the machine for support.
- Use strict form. Raise the weight using thigh power only. Bring your legs upwards in a wide arc, until they are past parallel to the floor.
- Pause to tense and squeeze your thighs.
- Lower the weight down slowly and with control, fighting gravity all the way to get the benefit of negative resistance.
- Stay tight throughout the movement. Use deep concentration, and go for the burn!

TIPS: To work the outer quads, point your toes out and in line with your thighs throughout the set. To work the inner quads, point your toes up (at right angles to the thighs) and in. If the pad is wide enough, you can also work the inner or outer quads more by using a narrow or wide foot placement, with the feet positions as recommended.

73

Start

Hamstrings (or "Leg Biceps")

Lying Leg Curls

GOAL: To work and isolate the hamstrings. Some glutes are also involved, but lower-back and hip involvement should be kept to a minimum.

COMMON MISTAKES: Swinging the weight up and dropping it down without resisting gravity; and raising the hips off the bench and hunching the weight up with the help of the glutes, lower back, and hips. These problems commonly occur from trying to use too much weight.

NOTE: For most beginners, this is a strict-form isolation exercise, not a power movement. For this reason, moderate weights and higher repetitions (12 to 20 reps) are recommended until some strength and development are attained.

Description:

• Lie facedown on the leg-curl bench, positioning the pad across your ankles.

• Rest your upper torso on your elbows, keeping your hips down and low.

• Maintain an arch in your lower back.

• Press your hips into the bench, and keep them there throughout the set. Do not let your hips or glutes get involved in raising the weight; make it pure leg-biceps power.

• Raise the weight until your lower legs are horizontal to your body, or a little past horizontal. Pause to tense and squeeze your leg biceps.

• Lower the weight with control, not letting your legs straighten completely at the bottom. You keep better tension on your leg biceps if you maintain a little bend in your knees.

• Fight gravity to get the benefit of negative resistance.

TIPS: Pointing your toes throughout the set allows you to isolate your lower-leg biceps better, though you might have to use less weight. Using wide or narrow foot placement and pointing your toes in or out helps to work the inner or outer hamstrings more. If you have trouble keeping your hips down, have your training partner push down on your hips/glutes until you feel the correct form.

Finish

Standing Leg Curls

GOAL: To isolate the hamstrings, or leg biceps.

COMMON MISTAKES: Leaning too far forward and raising the weight with glute/lower-back power. This often comes from trying to use too much weight for good form. Use moderate weights and higher reps.

Description:

- Place your foot in the foot support. Maintain an erect torso, and raise the weight by bending your knee at a right angle.
- Pause to tense and squeeze your hamstring for a second or two.
- Only your lower leg should move.
- Lift the weight explosively on the positive; resist slowly all the way down on the negative.
- Always maintain a little bend in your knee at the bottom, to better keep tension on your leg biceps.
- Repeat for the desired number of reps, and then alternate your legs.

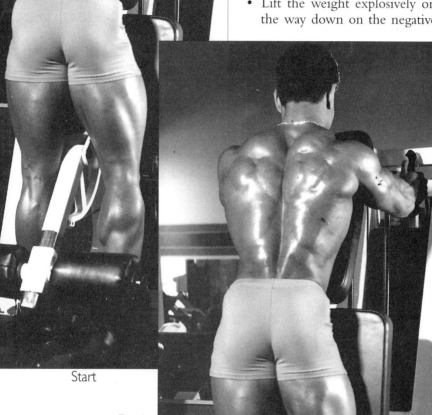

Start

Finish

Calves

Start

Standing Calf Raises

GOAL: To work the gastrocnemius muscle of the calves.

COMMON MISTAKES: Using too much weight and too short a range of motion (many bodybuilders use short bouncing reps and never give their calves a proper stretch); rolling over on the outer side of the foot instead of putting the pressure on the big toe, as one ascends to the top position.

NOTE: The calves are composed of mainly red "slow-twitch" muscle fibers. Because we walk on our calves, Mother Nature made it very difficult to properly fatigue the calf muscles. For this reason, calf exercises should be performed with high reps—anywhere from 15 to 100 reps per set (the latter only for shocking purposes). For most sets, 15 to 30 reps should suffice.

Description:

Finish

• Set the pin selector in the weight stack of the machine at a weight that comfortably allows 20 reps the first set.

• Get into position on a standing-calf machine by bending your knees and placing the shoulder pads comfortably on your shoulders. Set your feet less than shoulders'-width apart, your toes pointing straight ahead.

• Make sure you're standing on a block a minimum of 4 inches high—preferably 6 inches. One covered in gum rubber is best, because it prevents the feet from sliding and pads the feet. The best calf blocks are curved to allow the balls of the feet to act as a fulcrum.

• When you're ready to begin, straighten your knees. Push up with calf power, rising as high as possible. At the top, all the pressure should be on the big toes. Pause for a brief second to contract the calves.

• Lower down slowly and with control. Do not just drop down and bounce. Focus on lowering your heels as low as possible, while at the same time building up tension in your calves from the stretch. Don't start back up until you've finished going all the way down.

• When your heels will go no lower, push up as high as you can, again putting the pressure on the big toes at the top.

• Repeat for high reps. At the end, do some short, burning, bouncing reps to put extra tension on the calves.

TIPS: Many bodybuilders like to turn their toes in and out to work the inner and outer heads of the gastrocnemius. Other experts, such as John Parrillo, recommend twisting the heels in at the top, to work the inner head, and twisting the heels out at the top, to work the outer head. Using a wide stance, so that the foot naturally rolls over on the outer edge, also helps work the outer head.

Seated Calf Raises

Start

GOAL: To work the soleus of the calves, the part of the calf that lies beneath the gastrocnemius. In order to work the soleus, the knees must be bent at a right angle.

COMMON MISTAKES: Not using a full enough range of motion; not getting enough stretch at the bottom; using too much inertia and momentum, and not enough muscle power, by performing short, bouncing reps.

NOTE: The soleus is even more difficult to fatigue than the gastrocnemius, so even higher reps are recommended—say, 25 to 50 reps for most sets, and occasionally going up to 100 reps.

Description:

- Sit down and place the pads of the seated-calf machine comfortably and evenly across your knees to distribute the load evenly.

- Release the lever. Lift your heels as high as possible, placing emphasis on the big toes in the top, fully contracted position.

- Focus on lowering your heels slowly as far down as possible. Feel the tension build in your calves, as they are stretched more and more. When your heels can go no lower, push up hard and rise as high as possible on your big toes. Hold and contract your calves.

- Lower and repeat.

TIPS: Turning your toes in or out can put more pressure on the inside and outside heads, as can twisting your heels in or out at the top. To work the outer heads, assume a very wide stance so that the stress will naturally go to the outside head.

Finish

Abdominals (or "Abs")

Crunches

GOAL: To work the rectus abdominus muscles, sometimes called the upper abs.

COMMON MISTAKES: Performing the movement too fast; failing to contract the abs on each rep; placing too much strain on the neck by pulling on the back of the head with the hands.

Description:
- Lie on your back, with your legs draped over a low, flat bench. Your hips and knees should form right angles to the floor. Place your hands behind your head for support. Maintain the right angles of the hips and knees throughout the set.

- Imagine that your torso is a roll of carpet, and roll the carpet up by slowly and deliberately raising your shoulders off the ground. The lower back stays in contact with the floor/mat at all times. Keep your hands relaxed, and don't push with your neck.

- As your shoulders come up, "crunch" your abdominal muscles for a count of two. It helps to think of "crunching" or squeezing the abs between the thighs and the torso. Then slowly return to the starting position.

- Repeat until the abs are fatigued and burning.

Finish

Twisting Crunches

GOAL: To work the intercostal muscles on the side of the waist, along with some abdominal stimulation.

COMMON MISTAKES: Straining the neck by pulling too hard with the hands; failing to contract the muscles during each rep; not using enough concentration.

Description:

- Lie on the floor, with your knees bent and your feet flat on the floor. Put your hands behind your neck, keeping your elbows wide apart. Keep your hands relaxed.

- Slowly raise your right shoulder and upper back off the floor, along with your right hip a little, too. Twist your shoulder towards your left knee. Pause to squeeze and "crunch" the muscles, waiting to feel the contraction before lowering to the floor.

- Alternate sides (left shoulder to right knee).

Start

Finish

Hanging Knee Raises

GOAL: To work the lower abdominals.

COMMON MISTAKES: Hanging from the chinning bar with the back straight, the pelvis tilted back, the lower back arched, and the knees locked and the legs straight. Lifting the legs in this manner works the hips and pelvis rather than the abdominals.

Start

Finish

Description:

- Take a slightly wider than shoulders'-width grip on the bar. Use straps to reinforce your grip if possible. If straps are not available, at least use sponges to prevent your hands from slipping. Some gyms have arm slings that can be used on chinning bars that fit under the armpits to support the body. This way, grip is not involved, so all concentration can be kept on working the abs.

- To properly isolate the abs, it is necessary to rock the pelvis forward and maintain a forward pelvis tilt throughout the exercise. To help maintain this crucial position, round or hunch your back, making your body form a "quarter moon" or the letter "U" tilted.

- Tilt your head forward until your chin touches your chest. Do not keep it upright or tilted backwards.

- Bend your knees, and raise them until they almost touch your chest. Hold and "crunch" and squeeze your abs until they contract.

- Perform the reps slowly and with control, deliberation, and concentration.

- Focus on performing one correct rep at a time. One good rep is better than five sloppy ones.

- Lower your knees with control to take advantage of negative resistance. Feel the stretch in your abs as you do.

- Do not straighten your legs all the way at the bottom; always maintain some bend in your knees.

- Repeat until your abs are fatigued.

Start

Finish

Seated Bench Leg Tucks

GOAL: To isolate the lower abdominals.

COMMON MISTAKES: Sitting too upright; the back not hunched or bowed in the "quarter moon" position; failing to contract the abs on each rep; allowing the feet to hit the floor and taking tension off the abs; allowing the legs to completely straighten in the bottom position.

Description:

- Sit at the edge of a flat bench. Extend your legs out in front of you, keeping some bend in your knees. Grasp the sides of the bench with your hands to maintain your balance.

- As you extend your legs, arch your back.

- As you bring your knees to your body, allow your knees to bend at right angles to your body. Try to bring your knees to your chest.

- As your knees touch your body, hunch (bow) your back. Pause to "crunch" and squeeze your abs. Hold for a count of two.

- Extend your legs to the starting position and repeat.

- Perform the reps with tempo, but don't do them so fast that you lose control or fail to contract your abs each rep.

Start

Traps

Barbell Shrugs

GOAL: To work the large trapezius muscle of the upper back.

COMMON MISTAKE: Using too much weight and too short a range of motion. Many bodybuilders do short bouncing reps with very heavy weights, which puts tremendous strain on the connective tissue.

Finish

NOTE: This exercise is best done in a power rack with the safety racks set at midthigh point, or using a Smith machine, the bench-press station of a Universal machine, or a special shrugging machine. It can also be done one dumbbell at a time, which allows for greater range of motion.

Description:

• Set a heavy barbell in a power rack at midthigh level.

• Take a shoulders'-width grip. Use straps or sponges to reinforce your grip.

• Lift the weight using just the strength of your traps. Do not bend your arms, and do not bounce the weight at the bottom (rebound).

• Try to touch your shoulders to your ears and hold for a count of two, while tensing and squeezing your traps.

• Lower and repeat.

Start

Power Cleans

GOAL: To develop the traps and upper-back thickness and muscularity. The biceps and lower back also get a good workout.

COMMON MISTAKES: Not knowing how to clean the bar to the shoulders properly (have an experienced lifter show you how if you're not sure); dipping under the weight; keeping the legs locked while cleaning, and rounding the back; using too much weight and losing control.

Description:

- Choose a weight that allows between 6 and 10 reps.
- Take a shoulders'-width (or slightly wider) over-hand grip on the bar. Use straps or sponges to reinforce your grip.
- Bend over at your waist, arms at full length, keeping your knees slightly bent.
- The back is flat, the lower back is arched, with your head up. Don't allow your lower back to round or your back to hump over.
- The glutes are low, so your back is inclined at about a 45° angle. In many ways, the start of the clean is similar to the start of the regular barbell deadlift.
- In one motion, clean the bar to your shoulders, with little dipping under the weight.
- Lower the weight carefully to the starting position and repeat.

Finish

- Many lifters favor an over/under grip; that is, their strongest hand holds the bar with a curl grip, their weaker hand with an overhand grip. Use sponges or straps to reinforce your grip. Make sure your grip is balanced properly.

- Many of the initial body placements are similar to those of the power clean. Bend at your hips, keep your lower back arched, your back flat, your hips and glutes low.

- With your arms extended and your head up, bend at the knees. With your back flat and inclined at about a 45° angle, and your lower back arched, begin to pull the weight off the ground.

- Once the bar gets to your knees, your legs should straighten to help drive the bar up. Keep that lower back arched; don't let it round, or you'll invite a lower-back injury.

- Keep pulling until the bar is at midthigh height; the arms are extended, and the upper body is erect.

- Lower carefully and with control, and repeat.

Deadlift

GOAL: To develop the lower and middle back, although the grip, glutes, hamstrings, and traps get work, too. The deadlift develops tremendous overall body power.

COMMON MISTAKE: The biggest mistake is rounding the back and pulling too much with the arms, instead of lifting with the large muscles of the back.

NOTE: This is a low- to moderate-rep power movement. Keep reps in the 6 to 8 range, and once a month pyramid down to one or two reps.

Description:
- Choose a weight that allows a comfortable 8 reps in the first set. Make sure you're well warmed up before attempting heavy weights.

- Bend over the bar and grasp it using a shoulders'-width (or slightly wider) grip.

Finish

Latissimus Dorsi Muscles (or "Lats")

Wide-Grip Chins

GOAL: To work the outer sections of the lats. To spread the scapulae and create upper-back and lat width.

NOTE: The wide-grip chin is probably the number-one lat developer. The wide-grip lat pulldown is a poor substitute. Chins should always be the chief exercise in any lat routine. Even if you're not very strong and can't do many chins, always include it in your routine and try to do as many reps as possible, adding a rep or two per set every week or so. Challenge yourself to get to the point where you can do at least 20 consecutive wide-grip chins.

COMMON MISTAKES: Wrapping the fingers around the chinning bar and pulling too much with the hands and biceps; failing to arch the chest, drop the shoulders, and maintain an arched lower back; kicking with the legs to help reach the bar; dropping down quickly without resisting gravity, which eliminates negative resistance; using too wide a grip.

Start

Description:

- Stand on a box or bench that allows you to get a good grip on the bar.
- Take an overhand grip on the chin bar. Use straps or sponges to reinforce your grip. The grip should be several inches wider than shoulders' width but not as wide as your hands will go. Gripping where most chinning bars begin to bend or curve seems to be about the right width for most people. Make sure the grip is evenly spaced.
- The higher you place your hands on the bar, the less involvement of the biceps, and the more the lats pull out. There is a trade-off, however, as such a grip can cause more strain on the wrists. Find the ideal compromise.
- Once you've secured your grip, step off the box and hang free.
- Expand your chest, arch your rib cage, and drop your shoulders back.
- Keep your elbows wide apart.
- Pull yourself up smoothly (no leg kicking), until your chin is above bar level. Pause briefly to tense and squeeze your lats.
- As you pull yourself up, pull your elbows in close to your body.
- Lower slowly and with control, feeling the stretch in your lats as you descend. You should also feel your lats spread at the same time.
- Always maintain a bit of bend in your elbows at the bottom to keep more tension on your lats.
- Repeat for as many reps as possible.

Finish

Bent-Over Barbell Rows

GOAL: To thicken the lats and develop midback thickness. The biceps, grip, and upper back get some stimulation as well.

COMMON MISTAKES: Number one is rounding the back. The lats cannot contract when the lower back rounds, so maintain an arched lower back at all times. The other common mistakes are ducking the head down, which forces the glutes and hips too high, and using speed and momentum to yank the bar up, instead of pulling smoothly with lat power. When form gets really sloppy, people are forced to drop their chest to meet the bar, and they even stand up with the weight, deadlift–style, instead of rowing the bar. All these mistakes occur from using too much weight. Other mistakes are using too short a range of motion, pulling with the hands too much, and rowing on a 90° plane of motion.

NOTE: Barbell rowing can be performed with either an overhand or curl grip. The curl grip is better for low-lat development, and is a favorite of Dorian Yates, Michael Francois, and Jim Quinn.

Start

Finish

Description:

- A little imagery might help you better understand the necessary body positions for good barbell rowing. Visualize a jet plane coming in for a landing: The nose is high, the tail is low, the wheels are down, and the flaps are down. Make your body like the jet plane. The head is high, the glutes and hips are lower than the upper body, and the back is flat and on approximately a 45° angle, with the lower back arched. You should feel as if you are sitting down as you row the bar, because of the flexed knees and low glutes.

- Make sure your grip is evenly spaced. Use straps or sponges to reinforce your grip.

- Bend over at the waist, holding the bar at arms' length. Assume the positions as described. Your torso should be tilted, because of the low-glute position, and above parallel to the floor.

- Pull the bar on a tilted plane into your lower abdominal region. Pull your elbows up and back as far as you can. At the top, tense and squeeze your lats.

- Lower the bar down slowly with control, feeling your lats spread and stretch all the way. Don't just drop the bar down or try to rebound it up from the bottom position. The bar actually moves down and away from the body a little, not just straight down.

- Don't start up until you've finished going all the way down. Only when your lats are stretched fully should you start another rep.

Start

Finish

Single-Arm Dumbbell Rowing

GOAL: To work the lower lats, especially where they insert at the bottom.

COMMON MISTAKES: Heaving the dumbbell up and down, instead of rowing it with control; dropping the dumbbell from the top, which eliminates negative resistance; not getting a contraction at the top; not getting a proper stretch at the bottom; lifting the bell straight up and down, which works the rear delts, traps, and rhomboids too much, and the lats not enough.

Description:

- To row with your right arm, kneel with your left leg on a flat bench, your right leg extended behind your body.

- Hold a medium-heavy dumbbell in your right hand, the palm facing towards your body. Use straps or sponges to reinforce your grip.

- As you lower the dumbbell, also reach out and away from your body, so that the dumbbell moves in a "sawing wood" motion. Near the bottom of the range of motion, twist your wrist so that your knuckles now face forward. Feel the stretch all the way.

- When the dumbbell has moved down and away as far as possible, pull it explosively but with control on the same tilted plane to a point where the lower lats and abdominals meet. Remember to twist your hand going back so that your palm once again faces towards your body.

- Pull your right elbow back as far as possible, and tense your right lat. Repeat for the desired number of reps, and then do a set with your left arm. Alternate back and forth with no rest between sets.

87

Start

Finish

Seated Low Pulley Rowing

GOAL: To work the middle back and to add thickness to the lats.

COMMON MISTAKES: Using so much weight that you're forced to yank too much with the arms and use too much body motion to move the weight. Leaning backwards and going past parallel in the fully contracted position are the usual results of using too much weight. You want to come only to parallel and to maintain an arch in the lower back. Other common mistakes are to use only the arms to pull the hands into the stomach, and failing to arch the chest and drop the shoulders, which are necessary for proper lat contraction. Also sitting too close to the pulley, so that the plates of the weight stack touch, prevents the lats from stretching.

Description:

- Sit at the low bench of the pulley machine with your legs out in front of your body. Adjust the seat so that when your arms are fully extended, the plates of the stack do not touch.

- Use either a parallel grip with a triangle bar or an overhand grip on a straight bar. When using the latter, it's possible to use wide, shoulders'-width, and narrow grips. Whichever bar you choose, use straps or sponges to reinforce your grip.

- Reach forward to grab the handle. Your knees should be flexed, not straight. As you reach forward, your chest should bend over your thighs. You should feel a full stretch on your lats, but you shouldn't be so bent over that your lower back rounds excessively. Try to maintain the lower-back arch even when leaning forward, with the head up.

- As you begin to pull the bar to your lower-ab area, come to an upright sitting position. Do not lean backwards. Your upper body should be at a 90° angle to your legs and the bench.

- When the bar hits your abs, arch your chest, drop your shoulders, pull you elbows back as far as possible, and tense and squeeze your lats hard. Your lower back must be arched.

- Slowly let the weight extend your arms and pull your torso over your legs again to begin another rep.

- Repeat as before.

Finish

Start

more. Reverse-grip pull-downs are done to the front only and work the lower lats strongly. Parallel pulldowns using the triangle bar also work the lower lats strongly, and the serratus as well. Parallel-grip pulldowns with a wider grip can be done to either the chest or neck, and hit the fibers in a different way. Biomechanically, the biceps are in a stronger position when using a reverse grip or parallel grip, so heavier weights should be possible with these versions.

COMMON MISTAKES: On regular-grip (overhand) pulldowns, wrapping the thumb and fingers around the bar, which encourages pulling with the hands and biceps too much, instead of using a "thumbless" grip, with the thumb and fingers on the same side of the bar. The higher the thumb and fingers are placed on the bar, the less involvement of the hands and biceps. Other common mistakes are failing to maintain an arched lower back and pulling the bar too far in front of the body. Also, bending over in the fully contracted position, instead of maintaining an erect torso, involves the traps too much and doesn't bring about enough lat isolation. This usually results from using too much weight and not using strict form.

Wide-Grip Lat Pulldowns

GOAL: To work various aspects of the lats and upper-back muscles, such as the teres major and minor muscles, and the infraspinatus.

NOTE: There are many different exercises that can be performed on the lat machine for lats, depending on which type of bar or handle is used (straight bar, triangle bar, and parallel-grip bar): wide-grip pulldowns to the chest or to the neck, reverse-grip pulldowns, parallel-grip pulldowns, and medium-grip and close-grip pulldowns.

Each variation works the lats and upper back a little differently from the others. Wide-grip pulldowns to the chest work the outer fibers of the lats, including the belly and some of the lower lats, and spread the scapulae in much the same way wide-grip chins do; wide-grip chins to the neck work the upper lats, the terres major and minor, and the rear deltoid and traps

Description:

• To do wide-grip pulldowns to the chest, hold the bar at about where it begins to bend. Make sure your grip is evenly spaced (use straps or sponges to reinforce your grip). Remember your thumb and fingers are on top of the bar, not wrapped around it.

• Pull down the bar and sit down on the bench at the same time. Lock your thighs under the thigh pad to secure your body in place.

• Arch your chest, drop your shoulders down and back, and maintain an arched lower back. Tilt your head back, and pull the bar down and towards your upper-chest area on a tilted plane.

• Start to pull the bar down while simultaneously arching your back and thrusting your sternum (chest bone) to meet the bar. This means that as the bar comes down, you lean your torso back a little but still maintain an arched lower back. As the bar hits your chest, pull your elbows into your sides and back at the same time. Pause for a second to tense and squeeze your lats. Slowly allow the bar to return to the starting position, resisting all the way. Feel the stretch. The upper body should also return to the more upright starting position, too.

• Repeat. As you fatigue, it is permissible to use some body momentum to help drive the bar past the sticking point, but still maintain the arched chest, dropped shoulders, and arched lower back.

89

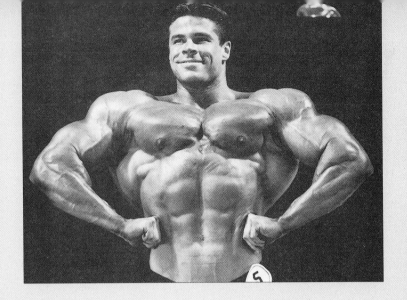

10

Endurance and Fitness

We do obtain a certain degree of fitness from training with weights, especially if we have a minimum amount of rest between sets of repetitions. Fitness is also improved as we increase the number of repetitions that we perform.

However, the essence of fitness is not associated very much with our skeletal muscles, but with organs like our heart and lungs. True fitness is gauged by our respiratory efficiency. That is to say, if our heart is strong (low pulses often indicate a strong heart) and our lungs can transport oxygen proficiently, then we are on the path to total fitness. Most sports give us a level of fitness, but, as you would imagine, some are better at this than others. Snooker, table tennis, baseball, and bowling do not compare as fitness builders to sports like cross-country skiing, swimming, rowing, or hockey.

Aerobic exercise builds fitness, and many aerobic sports can be simulated at any well-equipped gym. Using stair-climbing apparatus is not so different from hill or mountain climbing. The stationary bike is a perfect substitute for the mountain bike. In place of skiing, you can use cross-country ski machines, and using rowing apparatus can substitute for jumping into a boat and rowing upstream. Walkers and joggers can find machines that enable them to walk or jog as long as they wish without actually leaving the area.

Today's bodybuilders use "cardio" (aerobic exercise) to reduce body fat in preparation for a contest. Some bodybuilders, especially women, perform a cardio five to seven days a week. This, in conjunction with a low-fat, low-sugar diet, keeps them at a relatively low body-fat level all year round.

Most hardcore bodybuilders, however, only perform cardio six to eight weeks before a contest. In the off-season, they are often 20 to 30 pounds heavier. Invariably, there is a last-minute rush to lose this excess weight as the show date looms closer.

Does weight training help lose body fat? Only slightly. "Aerobic exercise, combined with a low-fat low-sugar diet, is the only way to strip off fat effectively," says Ms. Olympia, Rachel McLish.

(Left) Austria's Roland Kickinger. *(Right)* Jeff Poulin of California displays his mighty chest.

One man I greatly admire for his low body fat and high degree of physical fitness (especially since he is almost 80 years of age) is Bob Delmonteque, who believes in combining high-intensity weight training with regular aerobic exercise. According to Bob, "You increase the size of your blood vessels, raise your metabolism, strengthen your heart, increase the efficiency of your lungs, and generally improve the overall condition of your body when you follow a regular program of aerobic exercise."

You may be surprised to find out that your aerobic workouts do not have to be very strenuous to improve cardiovascular fitness. A study at the Cooper Institute for Aerobics Research determined that a 12-minute-per-mile walk increases your cardiovascular fitness as efficiently as a 9-minute-per-mile jog.

Even though walking can give you a fitness-building, fat-losing workout, for really effective aerobic training the exercise needs to be vigorous enough so that you're within 50 to 85 percent of your maximum heart rate (according to the American College of Sports Medicine). Your maximum heart rate can be determined by computing 200 minus your age. A 35-year-old, for example, would have a maximum heart rate of 175 beats per minute. If you wished to exercise at 50 percent of this figure (a good idea for the beginner), then your aerobic schedule would have you exercising with an elevated heart rate of 87 beats per minute. Naturally, as you become more fit, you can step up the intensity to a higher level. Beginners, depending on their current condition, should generally start with short aerobic workouts. A few minutes may be sufficient. Eventually, they can build up to performing 20 to 50 minutes of cardio four or more times weekly.

If you are over 35, a smoker, or have a history of heart or circulatory problems, consult your physician for advice before starting any aerobics exercise or nutrition program. This is for your own protection. Chances are, you will be given an enthusiastic go-ahead, but it's worth consulting your physician before throwing yourself into a program that may be too strenuous for you.

Taking your pulse is an important part of a cardio program. Place the middle fingers of your right hand across the underside of your left wrist. Move the fingers around until you feel your heartbeat. Count the beats for 10 seconds, and then multiply by six. Do not hold your breath, but continue to breathe in and out slowly. Perform several attempts if you feel you could have misjudged the count. Should you find that your heart is beating higher than your target rate, lessen your intensity immediately. By the same token, once you are into your cardio program, and your target heart rate tempo is down, you can safely increase the intensity of the aerobic exercising you are performing.

I would be remiss if I let you think that complete fitness can be derived from regular cardio training in the gym. There are many components to fitness. I truly believe that regular progressive resistance exercise (weight training) corresponds well with aerobic conditioning, whether it be working out on a jogging machine, a stationary bike, a stair climber, or a cross-country ski machine. However, none of the above will increase your ability to twist and turn for a tennis ball, fall professionally from a judo throw, or glide through the ocean like a seal.

Fitness comes from a variety of disciplines and skills. But did you know that hardcore bodybuilders, bent on maximizing their outer muscle mass, will likely hinder growth by trying to be good at all sports? Muscles need plenty of rest and relaxation if they are to enlarge regularly. On the other hand, if fitness, health, and endurance together with a functionally attractive physique are your aspirations, then spread your wings and be a jack-of-all-trades. The Mr. Olympia title will not be in the cards, but a lifetime of well-being and enjoyment is all but guaranteed.

(Left) Garrett Downing has built a great torso with consistent weight training. *(Right)* Deirdre Pagnanelli, Venice, California.

11

Nutrition

Volumes have been written on nutrition, but how complicated can it be? I mean, didn't the cavemen a zillion years ago know about healthy eating? And what about nature's animals, big and small? Each appears to have an inborn instinct as to what and what not to eat. Lions eat zebras but wouldn't touch a banana. Monkeys will go for a banana but not a pigeon. A hawk will go for a pigeon. But when it comes to us humans, we're all confused. Unlike Mother Nature's animals, we don't know what or how to eat. Heck, we even go beyond regular food and take supplements because we don't trust normal food to feed us properly.

Visit any grocery store. You'll find foods barely recognizable for what they are. Some have additives in the form of vitamins and minerals. Others have been deliberately revitalized to appeal to taste. How many foods can you name that haven't been altered by the addition of fresheners, color dyes, taste enhancers, and preservatives? Today we even have carb-free foods, fat-free foods, sugar-free, salt-free, protein-free….the list goes on. No wonder we're confused.

Everyone needs a diet that provides adequate amounts of energy (calories), protein, fat, carbohydrates, vitamins, minerals, and water. But, in addition, bodybuilders need to feed their body to adequately meet certain goals:

- They need to gain lean muscle mass quickly.
- They need to limit fat accumulation while gaining weight.
- Prior to competing, they have to temporarily reduce body-fat levels drastically.

Nutrition is a natural science, and, in order to succeed, bodybuilders have to use every bit of knowledge they can gain to increase their competitive edge. I have known men and women who have trained their hearts out in the belief that the exercise routine is the most important aspect of the bodybuilding process. In fact, it is the diet that is most responsible for dramatic physical change.

Unlike any other athlete, a bodybuilder has to eat sufficient calories to get through a regular day

(Left) Sue Price with her husband, David Fisher.
(Right) Geir Borgan Paulsen display his "cuts."

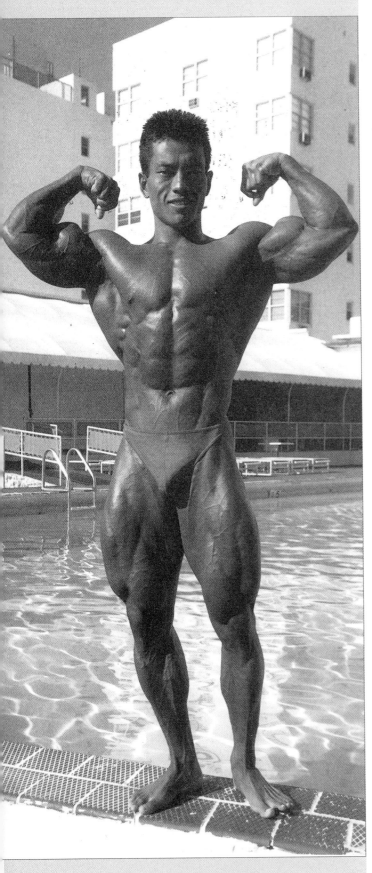

of living, working, and training, while, at the same time, taking in additional nutrition to allow muscle mass to store on the body, but not so much as to allow body fat to be stored. What a balancing nightmare!

Make no mistake about it, body fat is what kills your aesthetic appearance. Even relatively skinny people can look impressive if they have a low percentage of body fat. When we carry significant stores of body fat, our muscles just do not show up. They are hidden under the layer of fat, and their contours and profile are flattened considerably. It can be likened to a heavy snowfall over the Alps. All the cragginess and detail are lost when the snow fills in all the undulations of the mountains.

So, what should an aspiring bodybuilder eat? The first requirement is that your nutritional intake be healthful. You should never follow a diet that has the long-term effect of jeopardizing your health. This is usually not a consideration for the physical culturist, because it's necessary to eat plenty of food to build muscle mass. The only time when the diet could be considered moderately unhealthful is just prior to a contest, when the diet has to cause your body-fat levels to drop drastically to an unnaturally low percentage.

A very thin bodybuilder, with bony ribs and abdominals bursting through his skin, is fairly safe in eating anything and everything, although it is still recommended that the diet be based on predominately healthful nutrition. This means that deep-fried foods should be limited, and sugary cookies, cakes, and candies eaten only occasionally. Base your food intake on fresh fruits, vegetables, eggs, lean meats, fish, and whole grains. Your nutrition-breakdown chart should approximate the following:

Carbohydrates 55 percent
Protein 25 percent
Fat 20 percent

If you are already a seasoned weight trainer and have gained a noticeable degree of muscle mass and strength, then you should pay more attention to lowering your fat intake while keeping your carbs and protein intake relatively high. Also, your consumption of sugar or syrupy products should be minimal.

This stage of bodybuilding is your most important. You are building up steadily, and you have

(Left) Alan Ichinose. *(Right)* Australia's Lee Priest.

to maintain the progress. At this stage, you should no longer consume whole eggs. Opt for the egg-white omelet (cooked in Pam or in a nonstick frying pan). Eat chicken or turkey (no duck), but cut the skin away (however crispy and inviting) and, of course, do not add sauces or gravies.

The best vegetables to eat are potatoes (no butter or sour cream), cabbage, lettuce, beets, tomatoes, and broccoli (no avocados). The best fruits are oranges, apples, bananas, and berries of all kinds.

Eat whole-grain breads, oatmeal cereals, fish, and lean meats, such as pork, chicken, and turkey. Limit your red-meat intake to once or twice a week only. Some organ meat (heart, liver, kidneys) should be eaten once a week. Take in no added table salt or sugar—there are enough salt and sugars in everyday foods to more than meet your requirements. Lean towards nonfat milk rather than whole milk, although occasional whole milk is fine.

Fast foods and junk foods are invariably loaded with fat and sugar. Dairy products (creams, butter, etc.) should likewise be avoided. Also, steer clear of pastries, cookies, candies, bran muffins, french fries, pizza, and virtually anything that tastes gooey, sweet, and delicious.

The rules of your maintenance diet can be simplified to this: Eat natural foods, steam your vegetables or eat them raw, eat only fresh fruit (not canned), eat no fried foods, and cook meat, fish, and poultry without additional fats.

Fortunately, today ingredients are listed on food labels, enabling you to check out protein, fat, carb, and calorie content. It is not suggested that you try to calculate every last calorie or gram of protein, but a basic ballpark guesstimate can be helpful. It also might be a good idea to buy a calorie counter or small booklet showing the calorie and gram contents of a variety foods. There are some surprises out there. Did you know, for example, that most Cheddar cheeses are around 50 percent pure fat? That's bad news for any serious dieter. The same goes for your average bran muffin. A full 50 percent is fat!

Suggested breakdown for a seasoned weight trainer:

Carbohydrates 60 percent
Protein 25 percent
Fat 15 percent

The Precontest Diet

Even though you should be eating fairly clean in the off-season, your diet will have to change yet again if you want to obtain that ripped-to-the-bone contest condition. Clean foods are still the order of the day, but now you have to watch your consumption of natural sugars as well as fats. This means that even fruits have to be avoided or at least greatly curtailed during the last few precontest weeks.

Over the years, scores of precontest, or ripping-up, diets have been formulated. Many have failed completely. Today, through trial and error, most men and women who have to lean out for that competitive edge seem to follow a remarkably similar eating regimen.

The regimen consists of six "meals" daily of basically chicken, fish, or egg whites, with rice or baked potato. Other vegetables are seldom part of this eating pattern, but, if included (and they should be), they are usually broccoli, radishes, lettuce, and celery—all low-calorie items. This diet can get pretty boring, especially since salt and ketchup are definite no-no's. Liquids at this time are as important as ever, but they should be limited to noncarbonated bottled water.

Oatmeal can also be eaten at this stage, and is often the breakfast choice with egg whites, but beware of eating too much at any one time. Whole-grain breads and even low-fat muffins are not permitted during the contest-countdown period. Eating at restaurants during this time is also not permitted, because you can't be absolutely sure how their dishes are prepared, even if you ask.

The precontest breakdown could look like the following:

Carbohydrates 60 percent
Protein 30 percent
Fat 10 percent

Again, your nutritional intake is vitally important. How you balance it on a daily basis will make the difference in both your performance and your appearance. When I see a bulky bodybuilder lean out with a low-fat diet, I am totally amazed at the results each and every time. It's really quite miraculous.

(Right) Geir Borgan Paulsen gives an impressive lat spread.

12 Unsticking Sticking Points

t seems that most things take longer to achieve than we first imagined, including gains in bodybuilding. Even though early results are quite often remarkable, one can soon find that gains have stagnated, perhaps within a three- to six-month period. What do we do to jump-start our gains? There are options, all of which have proven to work well at one time or another, yet none are guaranteed to work all the time.

Bear in mind that we all have our genetic limitations. A highly motivated person who has been pumping iron religiously for 10 years, eating well, resting, and recuperating correctly may indeed be close to his or her personal limitations. Hey, it happens. If you are currently at a sticking point in your training, and believe in your heart of hearts that you can improve even more, then take a deep breath and plunge right in. I have always believed that no one has truly reached his or her genetic potential in this sport. There always seems to be room for improvement. Sometimes these gains can be quite dramatic, even among bodybuilders who thought that added gains were impossible. Below are some options.

Changing Your Workout Routine

If you have been routinely performing several exercises per body part and several sets for each exercise, consider changing things around. You could add even more exercises, cutting your sets to just two for each movement, or you could decrease the number of exercises and perform more sets of each. One common regimen used by former Mr. America Jack Delinger, in the early days of bodybuilding, was to double his normal number of reps whenever he found himself at a sticking point. Jack contended that the change in the number of reps invariably stimulated his muscles into growing again. After two weeks or so of high-rep training, Jack would drop back to his regular rep pattern of 8 to 12 reps per set.

Another way to shock the muscles into new growth is to change around all your exercises. Adopt an entirely new routine. Instead of bench presses and

(Left) IFBB Masters Olympia Champion Vince Taylor has remarkable muscularity at 42 years of age. *(Right)* Tom Prince of Irvington, New Jersey, shows off his amazing triceps.

flyes for your chest, try parallel bar dips and cable cross-overs. Instead of squats and leg extensions for your quads, try hack slides and lunges. Get the idea? A brand-new routine can renew your enthusiasm and stimulate added shape and mass.

Taking a Layoff

A layoff is time without training. To some, a layoff is virtually unthinkable. Their enthusiasm is so high and working out so ingrained that any thought of not training is impossible to conceive.

However, layoffs can be useful. They can bring about a greater focus when workouts are resumed. They eliminate any overtraining symptoms and rest the body to ready itself for the next round. Layoffs refresh both the mind and the body. They should be roughly a week in length, two weeks at max. After a layoff, resume your training with a degree of caution. Do not start that first workout with all-out weight loads and teeth-grinding intensity. Take it easy. After a couple of workouts, you will be back to your old strength levels. From this point on, with the momentum gained from the planned layoff, you will zoom past your previous levels of performance and be able to make rapid results again.

Steroids

Taking steroids is illegal in the United States, unless it is prescribed for either illness or lagging libido by a qualified physician. In my 40 years of involvement in bodybuilding, I have made two observations about regular steroid use: It almost always works, and it's almost always dangerous.

There is absolutely no doubt that taking steroids hardens, builds, and strengthens muscles. Steroids are the nearest thing to magic that I have encountered. I have seen bodybuilding turn weaklings into he-men, but with steroids these same he-men became pagan beasts of pure muscle.

The sad thing is that long-term use of steroids causes a range of side effects, despite the claims to the contrary of drug enthusiasts. Long-term usage can cause sodium retention, acne, hair loss, gynecomastia in men (breastlike softness in the chest, often referred to as "bitch tits"), aggression, hypertension, cardiovascular

(Left) Nancy Lewis goes for it on the competition stage. *(Right)* Awesome is the only word to describe Canada's Paul Dillett.

disease, enlarged heart, virilization in women (voice deepening, facial hair, enlarged clitoris, and absence of menstrual periods), tendon and muscle tears, enlarged prostate or impotence in men, immune system suppression, insomnia, sterility, headaches, and cancer. Quite a list, and surely reason enough never to go the steroid route.

Power Lifting

We seldom see a successful bodybuilder who isn't immensely strong. Handling ever-increasing weight loads is definitely the way to gain both strength and muscle size. It is my opinion that every bodybuilder can benefit from a period of power lifting. A three- to six-month period of heavy lifting would do wonders for your basic tendon and muscle strength, and would stand you in good stead when you return to your regular bodybuilding routines.

You would drop your normal training exercises. A pure power-lifting routine, working each exercise once per week, would be all you would do. It is simple. Here's how:

MONDAY

Bench Presses	Squats	Dead Lifts
2 x 20 (Warm-up)	2 x 15 (Warm-up)	2 x 10 (Warm-up)
6 x 3	4 x 5	4 x 4
4 x 2	6 x 3	6 x 3
2 x 1	1 x 12	2 x 2
1 x 12		1 x 10

Changing Supplementation

Have you ever noticed the change in your hair when you use a new shampoo? The same goes for supplements. You can get a whole new reaction if you change around your supplementation regimen, because you would be shocking your system out of its complacency. We all get used to the foods we eat, the exercises we perform, and the supplements we take. Changing things around gives our bodies new direction, new stimulation.

Read up on the various supplement lines, and make some changes. It could make the difference. (More about supplementation in the next chapter.)

(Left) Milos Sarcev displays his ripped physique.
(Right) Paul DeMayo of Massachusetts.

13 Supplementation

What is supplementation? Is it really effective? Are the added results worth the added costs?

Supplementation, in terms of bodybuilding, is the taking of concentrated foods (vitamins, amino acids, micronutrients, proteins, carbs, etc.) to benefit health, strength, fitness, longevity, recuperation, muscle hardness, fat loss, muscle mass, and athletic performance. Supplementing the diet with concentrated food additives is also used and recommended for memory loss, hair growth, improving intelligence, alleviating stress—you name it, there's probably a vitamin for it.

As far as the bodybuilder is concerned, there are a zillion and one supplements to be considered. After the initial hype, however, there is usually a falling off of interest for many of these products. Typically, early university studies indicate that a certain substance (in a double-blind test, no less) has been shown, for example, to improve muscle mass while shedding unwanted body fat faster and…wait for this…up to 500 percent more effectively than anything previously available. No time is wasted by the various supplement manufacturers. The product is almost instantly made available through retail stores, catalogs, and mail-order outlets.

Perhaps I am being too hard on the manufacturers. Many do put out an honest product, and many claims are substantiated by authentic scientific studies and, more importantly, by bodybuilders themselves.

But there are charlatans out there. Recent random tests showed that in 20 percent of the supplements examined, the actual contents did not exactly match up to label specifications. Rip-offs are being perpetrated on bodybuilders at this very moment.

Protein Powders

What can supplements do? For example, a good protein supplement that is egg- or milk-based (this indicates that all the essential amino acids are present) can be a favorable way to give the body quick, efficient, low-fat, high-protein nourishment at a time when eating a meal is not possible or is inconvenient.

(Opposite) (left) Dorian Yates *(middle)* and Nasser El Sonbaty *(right)* at the IFBB annual Mr. Olympia contest. *(Right)* Toronto's Vicky Pratt.

Your main protein should be derived from natural fresh foods (chicken, fish, egg whites). But there's no denying the convenience of having a handy protein drink when the muscles need feeding. Never resort to taking high-protein pills (each pill has a binder or glue in it to hold the grains together). The best products are powders, and the best powders are those made up from whey protein as opposed to intact proteins such as casein.

Nutritionists have established a protein efficiency ration (PER) so that how well the product assimilates can be ascertained at a glance. The PER is based on egg albumin (egg white), the most assimilable source of protein available and 80 percent usable by humans. The protein content in milk is second, with fish and meat following closely behind.

Avoid buying protein products simply by the percentage of protein listed on the package. For example, a manufacturer could package a 100 percent protein product made of cellulose. However, cellulose cannot be digested, so the product would be totally unusable. A protein powder should be assessed and purchased according to its ingredients or PER.

Vitamins

We all need vitamins. Each has its own use in keeping the body functioning well. Without vitamins, our physiques would decay within weeks. The best way to get your vitamins is from vitamin-rich foods, such as fruits and vegetables. However, as a hard-training bodybuilder, you will need to make doubly sure that you are getting sufficient vitamins, to protect yourself from nutritional deficiencies that would adversely affect your training progress. A multi-pack vitamin kit is the best antidote to any possible vitamin deficiency.

Minerals

Minerals are relatively simple chemicals. Unlike vitamins, which are organic, minerals are dead substances that can be dug out of a rock. However, they are needed by the body so that we can maintain optimum health, strength, and efficiency.

No, we don't have to eat rocks to get the minerals that our body requires. A variety of fresh fruits and vegetables will do the job nicely. However, if you have been living on overprocessed foods, then change your eating habits now and take a daily multimineral supplement to get yourself back on track.

The following is a simple chart showing the essential minerals, their dosage, and symptoms of deficiency.

Mineral	Dosage	Symptoms of Deficiency
Calcium	800 mg	Bone weakness and disease
Phosphorus	800 mg	Muscular convulsions
Magnesium	800 mg	Growth retardation
Iodine	120 mg	Goiter
Iron	14 mg	Anemia

(Left) Kim Chizevsky. *(Right)* Edgar Fletcher gives a double-bi in the weight pen, Venice, California.

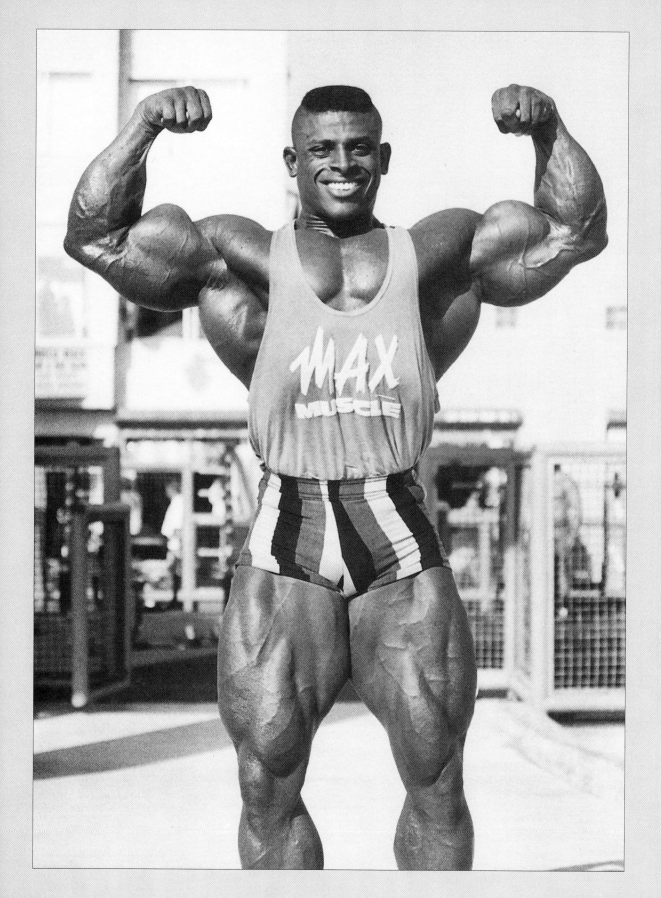

Amino Acids

These are the building blocks of the body. The first bodybuilder I ever heard of taking free amino acids was Vince Gironda back in the '60s. Frank Zane and Arnold Schwarzenegger were next in line. Today, many top bodybuilders supplement their diets with amino acids, although the craze is not at the level it was in the middle and late '80s.

Amino acids are found in high-protein foods, such as meat, fish, milk, eggs, and beans. They are used to build everything from your pecs and quads to your fingernails and hair. In all, there are 22 amino acids. Those that can be synthesized by the body are called "essential"; those that cannot are "nonessential." There are 10 essential amino acids, and 12 nonessential. Here are lists of both types:

ESSENTIAL	NONESSENTIAL
Histidine	Alanine
Isoleucine	Arginine
Leucine	Asparagine
Lysine	Aspartate
Methionine	Cysteine
Ornithine	Cystine
Phenylalanine	Glutamate
Threonine	Glutamine
Tryptophan	Glycine
Valine	Proline
	Serine
	Tyrosine

What added gains can you expect from taking amino acids? My answer has to be a little pessimistic. After talking to bodybuilders about the subject for 20 years (I found that 80 percent take amino acid supplements), I have received feedback to the effect that amino acid supplements only add a minimal amount of muscle size and strength. Their usefulness appears to be in their role in hardening the physique and in accelerating fat loss.

So, should you take them or not? If you need that added edge, and can afford them, the answer

(Left) Gerard Dente gives a lat spread for the camera. *(Right)* Olympia contestants Keven Levrone and Paul Dillett.

has to be yes. However, it is a good practice to first review your health status with a clinical nutritionist or a medical doctor with a knowledge of nutrition, because people have been known to have congenital amino acid and metabolism disorders.

Weight Gainers

Weight-gain powders are still popular among bodybuilders. Their main value is that they are usually very high in carbohydrates so that their calorie content is through the roof. Good stuff! Well, good for the really skinny guy who can't eat regularly. To gain weight, one needs to eat more than three meals a day; six to eight are nearer the mark. In fact, all bodybuilders, whether they are trying to gain weight or lose fat, should eat at least six times a day.

A weight-gain product (usually based on soy or milk powder) frequently contains fat and sugar to keep the calorie content high. If you need to gain weight, you should mix a weight-gain powder with milk and drink down a couple of glasses two or three times a

day. By all means, blend in some soft fruit, such as strawberries, blueberries, bananas, or peaches.

Caution: If you are inclined to be fat (or have a thick-skinned appearance), stay away from weight-gain drinks. They are exclusively for the skin 'n' bones types who badly need added pounds.

Become Informed

If you read through the muscle magazines, you will see page after page of hype ads for a variety of muscle-building supplements. Obviously, some of these products are better than others. But it's hard to say which are the very best, because a new supplement manufacturer seems to erupt on the market almost every week.

Read the ads carefully, and don't neglect to read books on nutrition, but always be a little suspicious. Science is improving supplements all the time. We are getting there. The best advice is to try the various supplements and see the results for yourself. When you find one that really works well for you, keep with it for a while and watch those muscles

14

Routines

(Left) Flex Wheeler of Venice, California, shows off his world-class torso.
(Above) Jean Pierre Fux performs a "most muscular" pose.

Every aspiring bodybuilder is looking for that secret routine, that combination of exercises, sets, and reps, that will jet him or her to a new plateau of strength and development. Bodybuilders are fascinated by routines. Whereas some star bodybuilders guard their exercise programs, most, in fact, will tell you about exercises freely, providing details about sets, reps, and poundages.

Champion bodybuilders all too frequently settle into a rigid routine once they have found out what works for their individual body makeup. However, minor changes are always being made. A few champions change their training programs completely, but they are in the minority.

There is no secret routine that works for everybody. There are too many other variables involved. Frequency is important. Intensity factors have to be related to your level of experience and your innate ability to tolerate strenuous physical exercise. Nutrition is another area of tremendous importance to the success of a bodybuilder.

The routines presented in this chapter are only suggestions. Don't feel that you have to follow them exactly. By the same token, don't add more exercises, thinking that the more exercises you do, the better your progress. The common mistake in bodybuilding is overwork, and many trainers fall into this trap. They start with a good basic routine. Then someone shows them a new chest movement, and they like the way it feels and include it in their routine. Next they read about a special shoulder-widening lift, a new abdominal exercise, and pretty soon their workout is twice its original length, and a definite chore to complete.

Typically, muscle enthusiasts will add exercises to their routines but be loath to drop any for fear of missing out on the benefits of a particular movement. This is a mistake. Long drawn-out routines are not the way to build muscle. Your aim should be to pulverize a muscle in as short a time as possible, then stop and go on to the next area. There are dozens of routines, but here are a few that have proved useful for many bodybuilders over the years.

Hard Gainer's Routine

Do you have a difficult time gaining muscle size? Hard gainers are frequently small-boned and have a limited allocation of muscle cells. Not all small-boned people, however, have a low number of muscle cells.

Frequently, a genetic superior can get away with eating junk food. A hard gainer cannot. A gifted bodybuilder can train haphazardly and irregularly—hard gainers cannot.

If you are a hard gainer, buckle down to a strict training regimen. Do not miss workouts, eat well, rest intelligently. In other words, you cannot afford to stray from the straight-and-narrow path necessary for bodybuilding success.

Hard Gainer's Routine

CHEST	SETS	REPS
Medium-grip bench press (elbows back)	5	6
Dumbbell flyes	3	12
LEGS		
Back squats (heels on block)	5	8–12
Leg press (45°)	4	12
SHOULDERS		
Press-behind-neck	4	6
Lateral raises	4	12
BACK		
Medium-grip chins (elbows back)	5	10
T-bar rows	4	10
BICEPS		
Standing barbell curls	4	8
Incline dumbbell curls	4	10
TRICEPS		
Lying triceps stretch	4	8
Close-grip bench press (elbows in)	4	10
ABDOMINALS		
Crunches	4	15–25

Executive's Routine

Office work can be stressful. It can also make you flabby. Weight-training exercises can help keep you both firm and fit. Do you want a steel worker's body, while working at a desk job? Good for you. According to statistics, if you are fit and strong, you'll do better in the boardroom, too. The sought-after image by corporate directors, executives, and managers is that of someone with a strong, virile body and an equally tough personality.

You may not have the time or inclination to build a Mr. Olympia type of physique, but the following routine will give you a body of steel, or something close to it.

Executive's Routine

WARM-UP	SETS	REPS
Stationary bike 12–20 minutes		
CHEST		
Medium-grip bench press	3	15
QUADS		
Hack slide	3	12–15
CALVES		
Standing calf raises	2	15–25
SHOULDERS		
Alternate seated dumbbell press	3	15
BACK		
Bent-over rows (barbell to waist)	3	15
BICEPS		
Barbell curls	3	15
TRICEPS		
Barbell triceps stretch	3	12
ABDOMINALS		
Seated knee raises	1	50–75
Broomstick twist	1	200
CARDIOVASCULAR		
Jumping rope (2 sets of 3 to 4 minutes each)		

Heavy-and-Light Routine

This type of training regime is becoming more and more popular today, as modern experts agree that there is evidence that training both heavy and light stimulates different fibers in the muscles.

Often, heavy training translates into multijoint movements, such as bench presses, dips, and squats. Light training is frequently the use of isolation exercises, such as thigh extensions and concentration curls.

The important point to bear in mind is not to confuse light reps with fast reps, in which the speed exceeds a certain rate and momentum takes over (and takes away from the usefulness of the exercise). Keep your reps under control, and make your muscles work!

There are two ways to use the heavy-and-light system:

• You can perform several sets of an exercise with heavy weights (and low reps) and then perform some lighter sets (with high reps) of the same exercise.

• You can perform a basic (multijoint) exercise using heavy weights, and then, after several heavy sets, you can change to an isolation (lighter exercise) and use high reps for 3 or 4 sets.

Heavy-and-Light Routine #1

SHOULDERS	SETS	REPS
Press-behind-neck	5	5
QUADS		
Squats	6	4
CHEST		
Bench press	6	5
BACK		
T-bar rows	5	4
BICEPS		
Barbell curls	5	5
TRICEPS		
Close-grip bench press	5	6
CALVES		
Calf raises (standing)	4	8
ABDOMINALS		
Roman chair situps	4	10
	4	50

Heavy-and-Light Routine #2

SHOULDERS	SETS	REPS
Press-behind-neck	6	5–6
Lateral raise	4	12
QUADS		
Squats	6	4
Hack slide	5	12
CHEST		
Bench press	5	4
Incline flyes	4	15
BACK		
T-bar rows	5	5
Lat machine pulldowns (wide grip)	4	15
BICEPS		
Barbell curls	5	5–6
Incline dumbbell curls	4	15
TRICEPS		
Close-grip bench press	5	4
Lat machine pressdown	4	12–15
ABDOMINALS		
Roman chair situps	4	10
Crunches	4	25–30
CALVES		
Seated calf raises	5	10
Standing calf raises	4	25–30

One-Exercise-per-Body-Part Routine

Save time with this one. You should train hard on each movement and limit your rest time between sets. It is important, when using just one exercise per body part, to make sure that the exercises selected are the best there are. In the following routine, the movements have been chosen that best work the belly of the muscle rather than just the upper or lower sections. This routine has to be performed at least twice a week.

One-Exercise-per-Body-Part Routine

CHEST	REPS	SETS
Medium-grip bench press	6	9
SHOULDERS		
Press-behind-neck	6	8
QUADS		
Back squats	6	6–10
CALVES		
Standing calf raises	6	15–20
BACK		
Wide-grip chins	6	10–15
BICEPS		
Standing barbell curls	6	8
TRICEPS		
Close-grip bench press	6	10
ABDOMINALS		
Hanging knee raises	4	15–20

(handwritten: 49, 60, 70)

Intermediate Routine for Aspiring Champs

If you are really serious about your bodybuilding, you do have to put in plenty of sets and reps, and you have to hit the muscles from different angles. The following off-season routine should be performed once or twice a week, but never all at one time. It should be split into sections. Concentrate on stressing the muscles when you train. Do not merely endeavor to lift the weight.

Intermediate Routine

CHEST	SETS	REPS
Bench press	5	6–8
Incline-bench press	5	8
Flat-bench flyes	4	10
Cable crossovers	4	12
QUADS		
Squats	5	6–10
Leg press (45°)	5	10–12
Thigh curls	5	12
Leg extension	5	12
CALVES		
Standing calf raises (machine)	6	15–20
Seated calf raises (machine)	6	15–20
SHOULDERS		
Press-behind-neck	5	6–8
Seated dumbbell press	4	10
Lateral dumbbell raises	4	10
Bent-over lateral raises	4	12–15
BACK		
Wide-grip chins	5	10–15
Lat pulley seated rows	5	10–12
T-bar rows	4	10
Single-arm dumbbell rows	4	10–12
BICEPS		
Barbell curls	5	8
Incline dumbbell curls	5	10
Preacher-bench curls (90°)	5	10–12
TRICEPS		
Close-grip bench press	5	6–8
Lying triceps stretch	5	10
Pulley pushdown on lat machine	5	12

Precontest Routine

You should begin a precontest routine 10 to 14 weeks before competing. It's best to make the switchover a week or two before you start your dieting, so that you are not overwhelmed by having to change your calorie intake and your training routine at the same time.

A precontest routine should include plenty of isolation exercises, movements that separate the muscles and "pop" them out when they are posed. Dumbbells and cables are used more frequently at this stage than during an off-season training period.

As you get into the precontest routine, it's a good idea to change over from working each body part so frequently.

Finally, you may experience some discomfort when it comes to energy levels and recuperation. If the discomfort is severe, take a day or two off and then resume training. It is important that you try to maintain good intensity during your workout. This will serve to keep muscle mass at a time when your limited calorie intake will be encouraging muscle atrophy.

Ron Coleman

Precontest Routine

	SETS	REPS
CHEST		
Bench press to neck	5	8–10
Incline dumbbell bench press	5	8–10
Flat-bench flyes	4	10
Cable crossover Superset	4	10
SHOULDERS		
Seated dumbbell press Superset	5	8
Seated dumbbell lateral raises	5	10
Bent-over lateral raises	5	12
Alternate forward dumbbell raises	5	12
QUA		
Leg press (45°)	5	10–12
Hack lift (knees out)	5	10
Leg extension	5	10–15
Lunges	4	12
Leg curls	5	10–12
CALVES		
Standing calf raises	4	15–20
Seated calf raises	4	15
Donkey calf raises	4	15–25
BACK		
Wide-grip chins	5	10–15
Wide-grip cable pulldowns	4	10
Single-arm dumbbell rows	4	10
Seated cable rows	4	12
Prone hyperextension	4	10–15
BICEPS		
Barbell curls	5	8–10
Incline dumbbell curls	4	10
Preacher-bench dumbbell curls	4	8–10
Seated concentration curls	4	12
TRICEPS		
Close-grip bench press	5	8
Triceps stretch	4	10
Triceps pressdowns	4	10–12
Parallel bar dips	4	12–15
ABDOMINALS		
Broomstick twist	3	200
Hanging knee raises Superset	3	hg20
Crunches	3	20
Lying half situps (twisting)	3	15
FOREARMS		
Reverse curls	5	10–12
Wrist curls Superset	5	10

Mass-Building Routine

Basic multijoint exercises should form the core of any size-increasing routine. They work the areas with large muscle mass. It might be a good idea to pyramid the weights when working on this type of program. That is to say, add weight for each set while decreasing the reps. This serves to thoroughly warm up the muscles for each movement.

As with most long routines, this program will work best if you split it into two parts, performing the first part on Mondays and Thursdays and the second part on Tuesdays and Fridays. Alternatively, you could split it in three parts and use the three-on, one-off frequency.

Most bodybuilders use a mass-building routine two or three times a year for six to 10 weeks at a time.

Mass-Building Routine

MONDAY AND THURSDAY	SETS	REPS
ABDOMINALS		
Crunches	3	20–30
QUADS		
Back squats	7	10/8/6/4/3/2/2
BACK		
Deadlift	5	6/4/3/3/2
T-bar row	6	10/8/6/4/3/2
TRAPEZIUS		
Shrugs (barbell in front)	4	10/8/6/4
BICEPS		
Barbell curls	5	10/8/6/4/4
CALVES		
Seated calf raises	5	15/10/10/8/8
Tuesday and Friday		
BACK (LOWER)		
Prone hyperextension	3	15–20
CHEST		
Bench press	7	10/8/6/4/2/2/2
Incline-bench press	4	10/8/6/4
SHOULDERS		
Press-behind-neck	5	8/6/4/3/3
Upright rows	4	8/6/4/3/3
TRICEPS		
Lying triceps extension	5	10/8/6/6/5

(Left) The remarkable Nasser El Sonbaty.

Pre-exhaust Routine

The pre-exhaust routine is entirely my own invention. I came up with the idea way back in the '60s, and subsequently published the routine in *IronMan* magazine in 1968. A pre-exhaust course was released in 1972, and ultimately I write the principles up in a book, *Savage Sets* (Sterling Publishing Co., Inc., 1989).

Sometime after I published the details of the routine, entrepreneur/inventor Arthur Jones built his first Nautilus exercise machine, incorporating the pre-exhaust system. My invention! Did he slip me a few hundred thousand for the idea? Not exactly. In fact, he didn't even try to contact me. But he did go on to gross in excess of $500 million dollars!

Be that as it may, I don't claim that the pre-exhaust method is the *only* way to train, or even the best method. It's merely a different way to train that you may want to try for a couple of months.

You can use the pre-exhaust routine for one body part at a time. You do not have to pre-exhaust every body part in your routine. In fact, to do so could well be too hard on the body.

How does it work? The method involves working a targeted muscle with an isolation exercise until it is tired or exhausted, and then immediately follow this with a combination movement.

Let's use the deltoids (shoulders) as an example. The triceps are involved in most shoulder-pressing exercises, and, in most bodybuilders, they are considered the weak link. This is clear when the press-behind-neck is performed: the triceps are worked hard and the deltoids are still relatively fresh. This means that your triceps will grow more than your deltoids. That's great if you have huge shoulders, but if you want to develop your delts more, then the best way for fast growth is to use my pre-exhaust method.

To get around the "weak link" triceps, isolate the delts first with dumbbell lateral raises (which don't involve the triceps). After pulverizing the shoulders with a hard set of maximum reps, go immediately into the press-behind-neck exercise, and again perform a hard set.

When you perform the pressing movement, the triceps will be momentarily fresher (stronger) than the deltoids, which are pretty exhausted from the lateral raises. You are no longer limited by the weak-link triceps. In short, your shoulders will be worked harder than they have ever been worked before.

The following is a sample pre-exhaust schedule for the total body:

SHOULDERS
Lateral raises (isolation movement)
Press-behind-neck (combination movement)

CHEST
Incline flyes (isolation movement)
Incline dumbbell press (combination movement)

QUADS
Leg extension (isolation movement)
Back squats (combination movement)

BACK
Nautilus pullovers (isolation movement)
Bent-over rows (combination movement)

BICEPS
Scott/preacher-bench curls (isolation movement)
Narrow-grip chinning the bar (combination movement)

TRICEPS
Triceps pressdowns (isolation movement)
Narrow-grip triceps bench press (combination movement)

CALVES
Standing calf raises (isolation movement)
Jumping rope (combination movement)

15

Questions and Answers

Father Knows . . .

Q. My father is very much against all formal exercise. He is especially against weight training. All he does is criticize me. He also says that all my muscles will turn to fat when I get older. Is he right?

A. It is physiologically impossible for fat to turn into muscle or vice versa. When or if you stop training, or if you stop playing a certain sport, then you should cut down on your food intake a little, because you are not spending so much energy and using up quite the calories that you did when you were more active. When you stop training, there will be a gradual return to how you were before you started, but in my experience no one ever quite loses all the muscle developed from regular weight training.

Training Aids

Q. I need advice. I went into a MuscleMag International exercise store in my hometown, and the place was full of benches, weights, exercise machines, stationary bikes, etc. But what I noticed most was the preponderance of small items like leather gloves, training straps, sponges, knee wraps, and belts. Do I need these items? Are they genuine training aids?

A. You do not need these items. Many people have built fabulous physiques without the use of any of these so-called "aids." However, some of them do have a worthwhile use, and can give you a training edge. Let's take a look at each item:

GLOVES

The only use I see for wearing training gloves is to avoid developing calluses on your hands. When Serge Nubret started training with gloves (he had a colorful pair of cycle gloves), we all thought he was a sissy at first. Then everyone started wearing them. I'll never forget seeing "animals" like Britain's Bertil Fox wearing gloves during a hardcore training workout. Here was a man who would grunt through the most gruesome workouts imaginable. The original "monster of muscle" wearing dainty calfskin gloves for every set of his training. I've noticed, however, that decidedly feminine Rachel McLish never chose to wear gloves during her training (occasionally she would wear them for a photo session, to dress

(Left) Sportsmanship is a part of bodybuilding—Vince Taylor and J. J. Marsh await the judges' decision.

up the photo). "I'm proud of my calluses," said Rachel. In truth, very few champion bodybuilders use gloves in their workouts.

KNEE WRAPS

Knee wraps are used as a training aid by hardcore bodybuilders and power lifters who have problems with their knees. Wraps also help a person to lift heavier weights. They are only used for squatting. The trainer wraps his or her knees prior to a set of heavy squats, and immediately at the conclusion of the set, they are unwound. The procedure is repeated on subsequent sets.

SPONGES

I very much believe in the usefulness of sponges. They are particularly helpful for all types of chinning and lat-machine exercises because they totally secure your grip (a very real problem for those with sweaty hands) on the bar.

WEIGHT-LIFTING BELTS

These wrap around the waist and are usually made of leather or nylon. Power lifters use belts (usually 4 or 6 inches in width) for all their lifts.

Bodybuilders tend to use them for exercises such as squats, deadlifts, rows, cleans, shrugs, and heavy overhead presses. A belt is not necessary, although it is easy to get into the habit of wearing one during the heavier lifts. There is no doubt that they do afford added support, but many people train without them.

TRAINING STRAPS

Chris Lund, a now famous bodybuilding photographer, was one of the first serious trainers to use training straps. He brought the idea from England to North America in the '70s.

Training straps, like sponges, are useful in helping the trainer hold on to the bar in exercises like barbell rows, chins, lat pulldowns, and deadlifts. They definitely allow one to achieve more reps. Because more reps translate to more muscle, straps are good news!

Best Trap Exercise

Q. A friend of mine told me that the best exercise for the trapezius is the bent-over barbell row movement. I need more trap development, but I was thinking of concentrating on the upright row exercise. Which is the better exercise to build the traps?

A. Neither! The traps are a huge muscle, best seen from the front as the sloping muscles that run from the lower neck to the shoulders. But the trapezius also covers a large part of the upper back and can be seen clearly from the rear, especially when the body is well defined with a low level of body fat. Bent-over rows do involve the trapezius, especially in the upper back, but the neck-to-shoulder traps (seen from the front) are affected mainly by shrugs and dead lifts. (The upright row exercise also works the area but not to the same extent.)

Shrugs can be performed with two dumbbells or with a barbell (held in front of the hips). Endeavor to touch your ears with your shoulders each rep. Try 4 sets of 10 reps.

The deadlift should be performed with a straight back and bent knees (head up). Try 4 sets of 5 reps. Neither exercise should be performed with heavy weights if you are not used to these movements. Start out light and build up the resistance as the weeks go by.

Arm Machines

Q. I am an experienced bodybuilder, but my arms have always been my weak link. They measure 17° inches, but, for my 6-foot height, I really want them to be about 19 inches or more. The gym I go to has a large variety of arm-building machines from the big-name companies, but my arms just won't budge. Any suggestions?

A. There are no really effective arm-building machines. Pressdowns on the lat pulley apparatus (which has been around more than 60 years) are the only machine exercise that really does a top job.

I suggest you keep with basic free-weight movements—two exercises for biceps, two for triceps—and then finish off with a high-rep super-pump drop set★ on the triceps pressdown apparatus. Try the following arm routine:

BICEPS
Barbell curls 5 x 8
Incline dumbbell curls 5 x 10–12

TRICEPS
Flat close-grip bench press 5 x 8
Parallel bar dips 5 x 12
Triceps Pressdowns 1 x 30–50

★A drop set is a high-rep set in which, after 8–10 reps, weight load is decreased, and then decreased a couple of times more after further reps.

Pump It!

Q. I keep hearing the word "pump" in connection with training. Can you explain exactly what this is, and how it feels?

A. If you got down on the floor now and did as many pushups as you could, you would get a pump. Your chest would feel warm and your pectoral muscles would be tight and full. This sensation, mildly pleasant, is the result of blood rushing to the area to feed and oxygenate the muscles.

At the beginning of his career, Arnold Schwarzenegger would delight in claiming that having a pump in the chest, delts, or arms was better than sex. He was exaggerating.

Loss of Mass

Q. I have always been active in sports—tennis, swimming, golf, running, skating—but now that I am in my sixties, I find that even though I am still active physically, I am losing muscle mass. In fact, I look exactly the same as my brother, who has always been inactive, a typical couch potato. Any suggestions?

A. Science has discovered that even active people will steadily lose muscle as they age. That is not to say that your fitness level drops. The only (and we repeat only) athletes who consistently hold on to muscle mass are weight trainers.

Strength training also helps women to avoid the bone loss that accompanies menopause. A 30-minute workout, twice a week, can help you keep your muscle tone and mass. Those iron pills are truly like magic.

Harmful Habits

Q. Are smoking and drinking really bad? How does cigar smoking compare to cigarette smoking?

A. Cigar smoking may be less harmful than cigarette smoking, but it is still a very dangerous habit. You should stop smoking immediately. There are no two ways about it. No one has smoked heavily and not suffered from it. Smoking always causes health problems, most of which result in pain, disease, and worse. Please take my advice and stop. After a month, you will not even want to smoke, and you will thank God you stopped.

Drinking is a different matter. Sensible drinking (one or possibly two drinks a day) is not considered harmful to the body. Heavy drinking, however, can destroy your life and soul, and is every bit as damaging as tobacco.

Hand Spacing

Q. Does it matter how far my hands are spaced apart when I perform barbell curls? I've read how a narrow grip tends to work the inner biceps while a wide grip focuses more on the outer part of the muscle. Is this true? I've watched a lot of professional and top amateur bodybuilders train, and they all execute the movement in their own unique way. Sometimes it seems as if exercise analysts are the most poorly developed athletes in the gym. Any insight would be greatly appreciated.

A. Understanding proper exercise technique is crucial to a bodybuilder's success, yet some do get a little carried away. Using a narrow or wide grip may work certain parts of the biceps a little more, but the difference is not substantial. Going to extremes either way may result in unnatural stress and potential injury. The best way to curl a barbell is with a grip most comfortable and natural to you. Simply stand in front of the barbell with your arms by your sides, and then bend over and clutch the bar at whatever point they come down. The space will usually be slightly wider than shoulders' width. A strong contraction felt in the biceps will ensure that you're doing the exercise correctly.

Elbow Pain

Q. I love heavy overhead dumbbell extensions but find my elbows hurt for a few days after doing the exercise. Is there anything I can do to alleviate the strain on the joint? I'm new to bodybuilding and don't know many different movements or variations of them.

A. I'm not a kinesiologist, but I have observed others experiencing the same type of elbow pain when using overhead dumbbell extensions in their routines. Doing the movement one arm at a time seems to present less stress on the elbow. You want a really good triceps isolator? Lie flat on a bench, and, with a dumb-bell held overhead, extend the weight across your body from the opposite shoulder. Use good form and moderate reps, and your triceps will fry! I find that manipulating hand spac-

ing when training triceps can drastically alter wrist and elbow strain. Don't be afraid to experiment and find what's right for you.

Bunch of Cheaters

Q. Living in Southern California, I've had the opportunity to watch a lot of professional bodybuilders train. One thing I've noticed is that almost all of them incorporate some swinging and cheating, especially on curl-type exercises. From reading the various muscle magazines, you'd believe that the elite of our sport always lift in textbook form with absolute isolation. What gives?

A. Most experienced lifters begin a set with perfect technique and, in an effort to increase the workload, add momentum (cheating) as their muscles become fatigued. Bear in mind that the "cheating" done by a top bodybuilder is far different from that done by an ignorant beginner. A pro will loosen the form as a way to prolong the set, but he knows how to maintain tension on the working muscle. Usually beginners cheat because the weight is too heavy and it's the only way they can move it. Veteran muscle builders know their limitations and don't need to show off.

Power-Packed

Q. I was recently introduced to bodybuilding by a friend and find the sport quite interesting. When I look at photographs of the heavily muscled IFBB athletes, I marvel at the kind of physical power they must possess. That much quality, grade-A beef must be able to move some impressive poundage. Am I right?

A. You certainly are. All that muscle is there for a reason—to lift heavy weights! I'm sure with a year of specific training, a number of heavyweight pros could destroy existing power-lifting records. Consider Arnold Classic champion Michael Francois. He's done sets of 5 in the squat with 735 pounds. He did this under normal training conditions without knee wraps or a power suit. (The two combined can add almost 100 pounds.) Now let's assume that when he's at his strongest in the off-season, he could power out a single rep in this manner with 800 pounds. I'd venture to say that with specific training for a meet, all the previously mentioned power gear, and a 12-week peaking schedule, Mike could squat close to 1,000 pounds!

That's just one example. Dorian Yates, Henderson Thorne, Kevin Levrone, Nasser El Sonbaty, Shawn Ray, Paul DeMayo, Greg Kovacs, Chris Cormier, among others, are all capable of exerting tremendous power. Taking everything into consideration, I'd say the top bodybuilders are the world's strongest athletes as far as actual muscle-contractile power is concerned.

Terror in the Trenches

Q. I have a real problem. For a year or so, I have been training in my basement on one of those multistation units, but decided recently to make the jump to a commercial gym. My enthusiasm quickly disappeared, however, when I started using free weights. They scare me. What if I can't finish a rep and get stuck under the bar? Or what if I drop a dumbbell on my toes? And before you suggest a training partner, forget it. I already have one. The fears are still there. My goal of climbing to the top of the Olympian mountain is vanishing as I write this. Could I just use machines and avoid the barbells and dumbbells altogether?

A. You have to take charge of the situation here. Guys have been hoisting barbells and dumbbells for years. Injury usually only occurs through bad form or lack of concentration—and you can count on one hand the number of people who've actually died in a gym through using weights. It just isn't possible to get where you want to be with these fears. Most physique stars have spent years pushing and pulling big weights with the blind aggression of a mule on mescaline. Shaking with terror when you grasp a 50-pound dumbbell isn't gonna get you far.

Give Me the Goods!

Q. I really want to get huge, man. What I need you to tell me are the secrets of bodybuilding. I know they exist. None of the magazines, including *MuscleMag*, divulge these training and eating secrets, but I'm hoping you'll come clean. You've been around the sport for a long time and know many of its legends, so don't try and talk around the subject. Give me the goods.

A. There really aren't any "secrets" being kept from you and the general bodybuilding public. Witness any professionals train, and you'll see for yourself that they do the same stuff we do. There are special

little techniques they may use that they've learned over the years, but the squat is always a squat and bench presses by any other name are still bench presses. Stop looking for excuses, and start busting your butt in the gym.

Skinny Legs

Q. I am a 26-year-old woman, and my legs are as skinny as the legs of a 10-year-old! My home-gym equipment has a leg-extension and leg-curl unit, but I can only lift about 50 kg. I've been on it three times a week training for two months, but I can't see any improvement of my legs. Why is that?

A. You must not give up so quickly. You've only just started! Add some squats and/or lunges to your program, and gradually try to work harder with a bit more weight or an extra set or two. Do not add weight too soon to your leg extensions and leg curls, but perform these movements more slowly, both up and down—down movements particularly (the negative part of the movement)—and feel the tension in those leg muscles.

Train your legs twice weekly with 4 or 5 sets of squats, 3 or 4 sets of leg extensions, and 3 or 4 sets of leg curls. Vary the number of repetitions, and throw in some lunges now and then instead of squats. Those legs of yours should improve in a few months if you stay consistent and serious with your training. Also, remember to eat protein to help the muscles grow.

Body Hair

Q. My problem is with body hair. I have just got into bodybuilding in a serious way and have been making great gains, which I am very happy about. But with all the will in the world, if you have body hair, you can't see the true definition you get from all your hard training. With this in mind, I have been looking for a solution in all the magazines—both inside and out of the bodybuilding scene—and have not been able to find any good answers. Bodybuilders don't seem to have any body hair at all, but that can't mean that they are all born hairless! I understand that there are medieval ways of getting rid of body hair, such as waxing and sugaring, but I can't believe that all bodybuilders do this. Surely there must be a less painful, more reliable treatment. Any suggestions?

A. You're right—professional bodybuilders are not hairless. And I'll tell ya, some of them (mostly the males) look like gorillas in their competitive off-season. If a guest-posing gig comes along, most of them simply reach for a bottle of Nair. If you don't like the appearance of body hair, you will have to spend a lot of extra time maintaining the smooth look. I can't comment on methods such as waxing and electrolysis because, quite honestly, I don't know much about them.

I suggest that you buy a good pair of clippers and run that over your body whenever you feel the need. Fine-tuning with a razor is an option, but again, you're looking at considerably more time. If having body hair is really a problem for you, then the time spent may be worth it. This is a decision you have to make for yourself.

Tattoos

Q. I am an 18-year-old male thinking about competing in a bodybuilding contest, and I want to know if getting a tattoo will hurt my chances of placing well. I've wanted one for as long as I can remember. I've noticed that certain IFBB pros, including Dorian Yates, have them. Please answer honestly, because I would like to go as far as possible in the sport. Thanks in advance.

A. Certain top-level bodybuilders do have tattoos, but I'm sure they'd have them removed if it were easy to do. A tattoo can only hinder a beautifully built body. It certainly won't help. Most of the pros you speak of try to cover them with makeup before they go onstage. Anyway, at 18 years of age, you're too young to make such a lasting decision. Believe it or not, you may change your mind about wanting a tattoo in the next few years.

Which Is What?

Q. What's the difference between mass, density, and thickness?

A. Mass, in bodybuilding language, is a term that refers to volume of muscle. Paul Dillett has mass. When a lifter has density, his muscles are packed so tight that they look like they're made of stone. Dorian Yates has density. Thickness can best be described as the look of power. Basically, thickness is only attainable through lifting ponderous weights. All the joints look heavy, and the body appears indestructible. Michael Francois has thickness. Personally, I like the combination of all three.

Music

Q. Can music affect the intensity of my workout? The gym where I train is less than hardcore, to say the least, and all they play is mellow music. I've asked for something more upbeat—and I've even brought my own music—but they refuse, saying the members don't want to hear that hard-rock stuff. Could I be getting better results with better training music?

A. I would have to say that music can have a profound impact on your workouts. Most professionals admit to preferring heavy rock when training. Energetic dance music also seems to energize a weight session. You have to remember, though, that most fitness clubs don't cater to heavy lifters. When choosing a workout facility, it's important that you take your needs into consideration. If there aren't a lot of options, you can't be choosy. Maybe all you need is a good headset. Some bodybuilders I know wouldn't go to the gym without one. If wearing it bothers you, then consider taking out a membership somewhere else.

Strength Loss

Q. Some days I'll have an awesome workout, and then the next time I train the same body part, I'll be as weak as can be! I don't understand this. Can my strength really fluctuate that much in the course of a week?

A. You have to remember that the human body isn't a machine. When a weight you lifted easily last week suddenly feels heavy, it's easy to conclude that you've lost muscle strength. In a way, you have, but the loss is only temporary. Your muscles haven't lost their ability to contract as forcefully as before, but unidentified factors have left them unable to operate at full capacity. The factors hindering success in the gym usually start with diet, rest, and stress levels; however, they become much more complicated when understood on a physiological level. We are never the exact same organism two days in a row. Nitrogen and glycogen stores, blood-acid levels, water retention, and a host of other conditions all fluctuate wildly from day to day. Your best defense against these variables is to try to keep your daily habits as constant as possible.

Tanning

Q. I'm a white male who tans very well. In four months, I'll be entering my first bodybuilding competition, and several of my weight-training friends have told me that despite my ability to achieve a dark natural tan, I should use skin dye. What do you think?

A. Believe it or not, I've yet to meet a white competitor who could tan dark enough to make the use of skin dye unnecessary. When you think you're sufficiently tanned after observing yourself in a mirror under normal lighting, you undoubtedly will still look too light on a bodybuilding stage. Heck, most black competitors aren't naturally dark enough! The average Caucasian male or female needs about four or five coats of skin dye over a good natural tan to achieve the desired look come contest day. Have a trusted friend paint you, and leave enough time for the job to be done correctly. Nothing looks worse than dye that has been applied sloppily with streaks and blotches.

Retaining Mass

Q. Whenever I see pictures of retired professional bodybuilders, I notice that, although they've usually shrunk considerably in size, one or two body parts retain much the same size and shape as when they were competing. This seems strange to me. Wouldn't the whole body atrophy equally when training volume and food consumption are reduced?

A. You're very observant. For instance, when Tom Platz retired from competition in 1986, took up running, and let his body weight drop, his titanic thighs still remained impressive. Arnold's biceps still elicit awe from moviegoers, even though he's physically a shadow of his former Mr. Olympia self. The reason? Genetics. Everyone has particular muscles that respond to weight training unusually well, and those body parts are also usually the slowest to return to their pretraining size. It's not fair, but the muscle you've put the work into building is the first one to go when you stop lifting weights.

Australia's Terry Mitsos

Index